AAT

Personal Tax FA 2016

Level 4

Professional Diploma in Accounting

Question Bank

For assessments up to August 2018

Second edition 2017

ISBN 9781 5097 1502 2

British Library Cataloguing-in-Publication Data
A catalogue record for this book is available from the British Library

Published by

BPP Learning Media Ltd
BPP House, Aldine Place
142-144 Uxbridge Road
London W12 8AA

www.bpp.com/learningmedia

Printed in the United Kingdom

Your learning materials, published by BPP Learning Media Ltd, are printed on paper obtained from traceable sustainable sources.

We are grateful to the AAT for permission to reproduce the sample assessment(s). The answers to the sample assessment(s) have been published by the AAT. All other answers have been prepared by BPP Learning Media Ltd.

Contents

Introduction

This is BPP Learning Media's AAT Question Bank for *Personal Tax*. It is part of a suite of ground-breaking resources produced by BPP Learning Media for AAT assessments.

This Question Bank has been written in conjunction with the BPP Course Book, and has been carefully designed to enable students to practise all of the learning outcomes and assessment criteria for the units that make up *Personal Tax*. It is fully up to date as at June 2017 and reflects both the AAT's qualification specification and the sample assessment provided by the AAT.

This Question Bank contains these key features:

- Tasks corresponding to each chapter of the Course Book. Some tasks are designed for learning purposes, others are of assessment standard
- AAT's AQ2016 sample assessment 1 and answers for *Personal Tax* and further BPP practice assessments. (The AAT sample assessment included in the Question Bank is a draft version. The AAT reserves the right to change the material.)

The emphasis in all tasks and assessments is on the practical application of the skills acquired.

VAT

You may find tasks throughout this Question Bank that need you to calculate or be aware of a rate of VAT. This is stated at 20% in these examples and questions.

Approaching the assessment

When you sit the assessment it is very important that you follow the on screen instructions. This means you need to carefully read the instructions, both on the introduction screens and during specific tasks.

When you access the assessment you should be presented with an introductory screen with information similar to that shown below (taken from the introductory screen from one of the AAT's AQ2016 sample assessments for *Personal Tax*.

We have provided this **sample assessment** to help you familiarise yourself with our e-assessment environment. It is designed to demonstrate as many of the question types that you may find in a live assessment as possible. It is not designed to be used on its own to determine whether you are ready for a live assessment.

You will receive a result for tasks 2, 3, 4, 5, 7, 8, 11 and 13 at the end of this assessment.
Equivalents of tasks 1, 6, 10 and 13 will be human marked in the live assessment.

Assessment information:

You have **2 hours and 30 minutes** to complete this sample assessment.

This assessment contains **13 tasks** and you should attempt to complete every task.
Each task is independent. You will not need to refer to your answers in previous tasks.
Read every task carefully to make sure you understand what is required.

Task 1 requires extended writing as part of your response to the question. You should make sure you allow adequate time to complete this task.

Where the date is relevant, it is given in the task data.

You may use minus signs or brackets to indicate negative numbers **unless** task instructions say otherwise.

You must use a full stop to indicate a decimal point.
For example, write 100.57 NOT 100,57 or 100 57

You may use a comma to indicate a number in the thousands, but you don't have to.
For example, 10000 and 10,000 are both acceptable.

If rounding is required, normal mathematical rounding rules should be applied **unless** task instructions say otherwise.

The actual instructions will vary depending on the subject you are studying for. It is very important you read the instructions on the introductory screen and apply them in the assessment. You don't want to lose marks when you know the correct answer just because you have not entered it in the right format.

In general, the rules set out in the AAT sample assessments for the subject you are studying for will apply in the real assessment, but you should carefully read the information on this screen again in the real assessment, just to make sure.

A full stop is needed to indicate a decimal point. We would recommend using minus signs to indicate negative numbers and leaving out the comma signs to indicate thousands, as this results in a lower number of key strokes and less margin for error when working under time pressure. Having said that, you can use whatever is easiest for you as long as you operate within the rules set out for your particular assessment.

You have to show competence throughout the assessment and you should therefore complete all of the tasks. Don't leave questions unanswered.

Written or complex tasks will be human marked. In this case you are given a blank space or table to enter your answer into. You are told in the assessments which tasks these are.

When these involve calculations, it is a good idea to decide in advance how you are going to lay out your answers to such tasks by practising answering them on a word document, and certainly you should try all such tasks in this Question Bank and in the AAT's environment using the sample assessment.

When asked to fill in tables, or gaps, never leave any blank even if you are unsure of the answer. Fill in your best estimate.

Note that where there is a lot of scenario information or tables of data provided (eg tax tables), you may need to access these via 'pop-ups'. Instructions will be provided on how you can bring up the necessary data during the assessment.

Finally, take note of any task specific instructions once you are in the assessment. For example you may be asked to enter a date in a certain format or to enter a number to a certain number of decimal places.

Grading

To achieve the qualification and to be awarded a grade, you must pass all the mandatory unit assessments, all optional unit assessments (where applicable) and the synoptic assessment.

The AAT Level 4 Professional Diploma in Accounting will be awarded a grade. This grade will be based on performance across the qualification. Unit assessments and synoptic assessments are not individually graded. These assessments are given a mark that is used in calculating the overall grade.

How overall grade is determined

You will be awarded an overall qualification grade (Distinction, Merit, and Pass). If you do not achieve the qualification you will not receive a qualification certificate, and the grade will be shown as unclassified.

The marks of each assessment will be converted into a percentage mark and rounded up or down to the nearest whole number. This percentage mark is then weighted according to the weighting of the unit assessment or synoptic assessment within the qualification. The resulting weighted assessment percentages are combined to arrive at a percentage mark for the whole qualification.

Grade definition	Percentage threshold
Distinction	90–100%
Merit	80–89%
Pass	70–79%
Unclassified	0–69% Or failure to pass one or more assessment/s

Re-sits

The AAT Professional Diploma In Accounting is not subject to re-sit restrictions.

You should only be entered for an assessment when you are well prepared and you expect to pass the assessment.

AAT qualifications

The material in this book may support the following AAT qualifications:

AAT Professional Diploma in Accounting Level 4, AAT Professional Diploma in Accounting at SCQF Level 8 and Certificate: Accounting (Level 5 AATSA).

Supplements

From time to time we may need to publish supplementary materials to one of our titles. This can be for a variety of reasons. From a small change in the AAT unit guidance to new legislation coming into effect between editions.

You should check our supplements page regularly for anything that may affect your learning materials. All supplements are available free of charge on our supplements page on our website at:

www.bpp.com/learning-media/about/students

Improving material and removing errors

There is a constant need to update and enhance our study materials in line with both regulatory changes and new insights into the assessments.

From our team of authors BPP appoints a subject expert to update and improve these materials for each new edition.

Their updated draft is subsequently technically checked by another author and from time to time non-technically checked by a proof reader.

We are very keen to remove as many numerical errors and narrative typos as we can but given the volume of detailed information being changed in a short space of time we know that a few errors will sometimes get through our net.

We apologise in advance for any inconvenience that an error might cause. We continue to look for new ways to improve these study materials and would welcome your suggestions. If you have any comments about this book, please email nisarahmed@bpp.com or write to Nisar Ahmed, AAT Head of Programme, BPP Learning Media Ltd, BPP House, Aldine Place, London W12 8AA.

Question Bank

Chapter 1 – The tax and ethical framework

Task 1.1

The tax year 2016/17 runs from: (insert dates as xx/xx/xxxx)

until:

Task 1.2

Tick to show whether the following statement is true or false.

Detailed regulations relating to tax law are contained in Statutory Instruments.

	✓
True	
False	

Task 1.3

Tick to show who the UK tax system is administered by.

	✓
Parliament	
Her Majesty's Revenue & Customs (HMRC)	
National Crime Agency (NCA)	
HM Customs & Excise	

Task 1.4

If you are employed by a firm of accountants, and suspect that one of your clients may be engaged in money laundering, whom should you inform about your suspicions?

	✓
HMRC	
Your firm's Money Laundering Reporting Officer	
National Crime Agency	
Tax Tribunal	

Task 1.5

This style of task is human marked in the live assessment.

One of your clients has expressed concern that his personal tax information may be disclosed to members of his family, who are also clients of your firm. He feels that this would compromise his right to privacy in his personal affairs.

Write a note responding to this concern.

Task 1.6

Tick to show in which TWO of the following situations an accountant is able to disclose information about a client without their permission.

	✓
If the client is unwell and unable to respond to HMRC	
If money laundering is suspected	
Where it would be illegal not to disclose the information	
If the information is requested from a 'connected person'	

Task 1.7

The five fundamental principles of professional ethics for AAT members are:

Use the letters in the left column as a guide.

I	
O	
Pc and dc	
C	
Pb	

Task 1.8

Tick to show who you should inform about your suspicions if you are a sole practitioner, and suspect that one of your clients may be engaged in money laundering.

	✓
HMRC	
Another firm's Money Laundering Reporting Officer	
National Crime Agency	
Tax Tribunal	

Task 1.9

Tick to show whether the following statement is true or false.

A non-UK resident individual is liable to pay income tax on their UK and overseas income

	✓
True	
False	

Task 1.10

This style of task is human marked in the live assessment.

A client has received a tax refund of £12,000 from HMRC. They were not due this refund but have already spent the money and asked you not to inform HMRC of their mistake.

What action should you take?

Task 1.11

Tick to show whether the following statement is true or false.

Tax avoidance is illegal.

	✓
True	
False	

Chapter 2 – National Insurance

Task 2.1

In 2016/17 Steve received the following from his employer. For each item, indicate whether it would be subject to Class 1 Primary, Class 1 Secondary, Class 1A National Insurance or none of these by ticking all the boxes that apply:

	Class 1 Primary	Class 1 Secondary	Class 1A	None
Salary				
Company car				
Mileage expenses paid at 35p per mile				
Bonus				
Department store vouchers				
Reimbursed travel expenses				
Private gym membership				

Task 2.2

In 2016/17 Iain received the following from his employer. Salary £27,000 (paid monthly), company car £3,000 taxable benefit, bonus in December 2016 of £2,000.

Show the national insurance that would be payable on these amounts.

(a) Class 1 Primary

£	

(b) Class 1 Secondary

£	

(c) Class 1A

£	

Task 2.3

Ann was paid an annual salary of £45,000 in 2016/17 and her employer provided her with a laptop for personal use only. The taxable benefit for use of the laptop would be £300.

On what amounts would Ann and her employer be liable to National Insurance? Please tick ONE box only.

	✓
Class 1 Primary on £45,300 and Class 1A on £300	
Class 1 Primary and Secondary on £45,000 and Class 1A on £300	
Class 1 Primary and Secondary on £45,300	
Class 1 Primary and Secondary on £45,300 and Class 1A on £300	

Task 2.4

Tick to show whether the following statement is true or false.

50p per mile paid to an employee for mileage would be exempt from national insurance.

	✓
True	
False	

Task 2.5

Tick to show whether the following statement is true or false.

Class 1A NIC is payable on vouchers given to an employee as a reward for working overtime.

	✓
True	
False	

Task 2.6

Wise Ltd has one employee, Freya, who is also a director of the company. In 2016/17 Wise Ltd pays Freya an annual salary of £37,000.

What are the class one secondary contributions payable by Wise Ltd for 2016/17?

Please tick ONE box only.

	✓
£987	
£5,106	
£3,987	
£2,106	

Task 2.7

What national insurance contributions are payable by employers and employees on a company car benefit? Please choose from the picklist below:

Employers	▼
Employees	▼

Picklist:

Class 1A
Class 1 Primary
Class 1 Secondary
None

Chapter 3 – Inheritance tax

Task 3.1

Identify whether the following transfers will be treated as a PET, a CLT or exempt for Inheritance Tax purposes in 2016/17. Tick ONE box per transfer.

	PET	CLT	Exempt
Gift of £100 cash to niece			
Gift of shares to a trust			
Payment of grandson's school fees out of income surplus to living requirements			
Gift of £5,000 to son on the occasion of his marriage			
Gift of £25,000 to friend			
Gift of classic car to spouse			
Gift of £10,000 to a trust			

Task 3.2

Norman died in May 2016. His estate was valued at £500,000. £100,000 was left to his cousin and the balance to his wife Maureen.

How much nil band would be available to Maureen on her death?

£	

Task 3.3

Identify which of the following debts would be deductible and which would not be deductible in a death estate?

	Deductible	Not deductible
Grocery bill		
HM Revenue & Customs – income tax to death		
Mortgage on home		
Illegal gambling debt		

Task 3.4

Tick to show whether the following statement is true or false.

PETs are subject to inheritance tax in both life and death.

	✓
True	
False	

Task 3.5

Tick to show whether the following statement is true or false.

A £5,000 exemption is available on any gifts given on a marriage.

	✓
True	
False	

Task 3.6

On 15 July 2016 Yvonne gave £500,000 to a trust for the benefit of her grandchildren. Yvette died on 27 December 2016.

What are the due dates for inheritance tax to be paid on this transfer of value? (please tick ONE box only)

Lifetime tax	Death tax	✓
31 January 2017	30 June 2017	
30 April 2017	30 June 2017	
31 January 2017	30 April 2017	
30 April 2017	30 April 2017	

Task 3.7

Bernard made a chargeable lifetime transfer of £260,000 (after exemptions) in August 2012. In November 2016, he gave £420,000 to a trust for the benefit of his son and daughter. Bernard agreed to pay any lifetime IHT due.

How much inheritance tax will be payable by Bernard on transfer of value in November 2016? Please tick ONE box only.

	✓
£87,250	
£69,800	
£88,750	
£22,500	

Task 3.8

Fred gives away shares in Fred Plc. On the date of transfer the shares were valued at 250–280p with marked bargains of 252 ,276, 264 and 279.

What is the value per share used in the IHT calculation? (show your answer in pence)

	p

Task 3.9

June gives 200 shares to her daughter – these shares are worth £3 each. June owned 500 shares prior to this transfer and the shares were worth £10 each. After the transfer June's remaining shares will be valued at £7.50 each.

What is the diminution in value of June's estate?

£	

Chapter 4 – Employment income

Task 4.1

Show whether the following statement is True or False.

An employee has a contract for services.

	✓
True	
False	

Task 4.2

Peter undertakes some work for XYZ plc.

Tick which of the following factors would indicate that he either has a contract of service with XYZ plc or a contract for services.

Factor	Contract of service	Contract for services
Peter is entitled to paid holidays		
Peter hires his own helpers		
Peter takes substantial financial risks when undertaking work for XYZ plc		
Peter does not have to rectify mistakes in his work at his own expense		

Task 4.3

Emma is employed as a retail salesperson and provides you with the following information about what she has received from her employer:

(1) Monthly salary of £2,000 paid on the first of each month until September 2016, with a 2% increase starting from 1 October 2016

(2) Commission of £1,000 earned during a special sales event in March 2017, paid with the May 2017 salary

(3) Employer's contribution of 5% of salary on 31 March 2017 to company's occupational pension scheme

(4) Bonus of £1,200 received 30 April 2016, based on company's accounting profit for the year ended 31 March 2016

For each item, show the amount that will be taxable in 2016/17:

Use whole numbers, and if the answer is zero, write 0.

Item	£
Salary	
Commission	
Employer's pension contribution	
Bonus	

Task 4.4

Show whether the following statement is true or false.

Tips received by a tour guide from customers are not earnings.

	✓
True	
False	

Task 4.5

A director of a company is entitled to a bonus for her employer's year ended 31 December 2016. The bonus is determined on 30 November 2016, credited to her director's account on 20 December 2016 and is actually paid to her on 6 January 2017.

The date of receipt of the bonus for employment income purposes is: (insert date as xx/xx/xxxx)

Task 4.6

Mo was provided with a petrol engine car by her employer on 6 August 2016. The car cost the employer £13,500 and the list price of the car was £15,000. The car's CO_2 emissions were 176g/km.

(a) The cost of the car in the taxable benefit computation is:

£	

(b) The percentage used in the taxable benefit computation is:

	%

(c) The taxable benefit on the provision of the car is:

£	

Task 4.7

Frank was provided with a new diesel engine car with a list price of £25,000 on 6 June 2016. The firm paid for all fuel (£2,300) without requiring any payment by Frank for fuel for private use. However, he was required to pay the firm £35 per month for the private use of the car itself. The car has CO_2 emissions of 153g/km.

(a) The taxable benefit on the provision of the car is:

£	

(b) The taxable benefit on the provision of fuel is:

£	

Task 4.8

Julian is provided with a company car for business and private use throughout 2016/17. The car had a list price of £11,500 when bought new in December 2015 although the company paid £10,000 for the car after a dealer discount. It has a diesel engine, with CO_2 emissions of 70g/km. The company pays for all running costs, including all fuel. Julian does not make any contribution for his private use of the car.

(a) The cost of the car in the taxable benefit computation is:

£	

(b) The percentage used in the taxable benefit computation is:

	%

(c) The taxable benefit in respect of the provision of fuel for private use is:

£	

Task 4.9

Sarah works for XXM plc, and is provided with a company car for business and private use throughout 2016/17.

The car has a diesel engine with CO_2 emissions of 209g/km. It has a list price of £57,000. Sarah agreed to make a capital contribution of £6,000 towards the cost of the car. The company pays for all running costs, including all fuel. Sarah pays £50 a month towards the cost of private fuel – the actual cost of private fuel is about £90 a month.

(a) Tick to show which percentage is used in the taxable benefit computation.

	✓
22	
37	
38	
41	

(b) The taxable benefit in respect of the provision of the car is:

£	

(c) The taxable benefit in respect of the provision of the fuel for private use is:

£	

Task 4.10

Francine is employed by Bale plc as a delivery driver and is supplied with a van, which she parks overnight at home. She uses the van to drive to the company's depot to pick up packages but otherwise is not allowed to use the van for her own private purposes. The company provides fuel for the van. The cost of fuel for driving the van from her home to the depot is £500 for 2016/17.

Tick to show the taxable benefit for Francine in respect of the van for 2016/17.

	✓
£3,170	
£3,768	
£598	
Nil	

Task 4.11

A camera costing £200 is bought by an employer for the private use by an employee on 6 April 2015. The camera is purchased by the employee for £50 on 6 April 2016, when its market value is £120.

The taxable benefit for 2016/17 is:

£	

Task 4.12

On 6 April 2016 an employer made a loan of £50,000 to an employee. The employee repaid £30,000 on 6 December 2016. The remaining £20,000 was outstanding at 5 April 2017. Interest paid during the year was £1,000. The official rate of interest was 3% throughout 2016/17.

(a) Using the average method, the taxable benefit for 2016/17 is:

£	

(b) Using the alternative method, the taxable benefit for 2016/17 is:

£	

Task 4.13

Tick to show whether the following statement is true or false.

If a loan of £7,000 to an employee is written-off and this is the only loan to the employee by the employer, there is no taxable benefit.

	✓
True	
False	

Task 4.14

(a) Vimal, who earns £30,000 a year, is given the use of a new television, costing £1,000, by his employer on 1 January 2015. Vimal subsequently buys the television from his employer for £100 on 1 January 2016 when it is worth £300.

The taxable benefit for 2016/17 is:

£	

(b) The television is used to keep Vimal entertained when living at 3 Sims Court, London EC1, a flat provided by his employer. The flat cost £120,000 five years ago when Vimal moved in, but due to a slump in property prices is now only worth £90,000. It has an annual value of £3,000. The official rate of interest is 3%.

The taxable benefit for 2016/17 is:

£	

Task 4.15

Giles receives a salary of £25,000 and has received the following benefits from his employer throughout 2016/17:

(1) Free medical insurance – the cost to the company is £385 per annum, although if Giles had taken this out privately he would have to pay £525.

(2) £55 per week of child care vouchers to be used towards the provision of crèche facilities for his child who attends a private nursery.

(3) A newspaper allowance of £20 per month.

Giles receives no income other than employment income.

The total taxable benefits for 2016/17 are:

£	

Task 4.16

Rita, a fashion designer for Daring Designs Ltd, was relocated from London to Manchester on 6 April 2016. Her annual salary is £48,000. She was reimbursed relevant relocation expenditure of £12,000. She was immediately provided with a house with an annual value of £4,000, for which her employer paid an annual rent of £3,500. Rita's employer provided ancillary services for the house in 2016/17 as follows:

	£
Electricity	700
Gas	1,200
Water	500
Council tax	1,300
Property repairs	3,500

The house had been furnished by Daring Designs Ltd immediately prior to Rita's occupation, at a cost of £30,000. On 6 October 2016 Rita bought all of the furniture from Daring Designs Ltd for £20,000 when its market value was £25,000.

Daring Designs Limited had made an interest free loan to Rita in 2015 of £10,000. No part of the loan has been repaid. Assume the official rate of interest is 3%.

(a) The taxable benefit arising in respect of the accommodation provided for Rita in 2016/17 and purchase of the furniture is:

£	

(b) The taxable benefit arising in respect of the relocation expenses is:

£	

(c) The taxable benefit arising in respect of the interest free loan in 2016/17 is:

£	

Task 4.17

Jon's employer provided him with a flat throughout 2016/17. The employer had bought the flat for £97,000 on 1 April 2014. The annual value of the flat is £800. Jon pays £100 a month to his employer for the use of the flat.

Tick to show the total taxable accommodation benefit for 2016/17.

	✓
£800	
£1,460	
£260	
£660	

Task 4.18

Petra uses her own car for business travel and her employer reimburses her 35p per mile. In 2016/17 Petra drove 13,000 business miles.

Tick to show what is Petra's taxable benefit or allowable expense in respect of the business mileage.

	✓
Taxable benefit of £700	
Allowable expense of £700	
Allowable expense of £1,300	
Taxable benefit of £4,550	

Task 4.19

For an employee on an annual salary of £27,000, tick for each of the following benefits whether they would be taxable or exempt in 2016/17:

Item	Taxable	Exempt
Interest on loan of £2,000 (only loan provided)		
Removal costs of £6,000		
Use of pool car		
Reimbursement of business expenses		
One staff party costing £100 per head		
Accommodation provided to employee who is not required to live in it for the performance of employment		
Provision of parking space at work		
Additional costs of home-working of £4 per week		
Long service award of £800 for 22 years service		
Accommodation provided to a caretaker for proper performance of his employment duties		
Work related training		
Provision of second mobile phone		

Task 4.20

Selina is employed by JKL Ltd. She gives you the following information about money she has received from her employer, and expenditure that she has incurred in relation to her employment in 2016/17:

(1) Annual salary £30,000

(2) Reimbursed business expenses of £600

(3) Employee's contribution of 8% of salary to company's occupational pension scheme

(4) Membership of professional body of £150 paid by Selina

(5) Membership of fitness club of £300 paid by Selina – she often uses the club to meet new clients

(6) £50 donation to charity each month under the payroll deduction scheme

(7) £1,500 expenditure on smart clothes to wear to client meetings

Using the proforma layout provided, compute Selina's employment income for 2016/17. If an expense is not allowable enter 0. Both brackets and minus signs can be used to indicate negative numbers (the expenses). Fill in all of the unshaded boxes.

	£
Salary	
Less allowable expenses:	
reimbursed expenses	
pension contribution	
professional body membership	
fitness club membership	
charitable donation	
clothing	
Employment income 2016/17	

Task 4.21

Lewis is required by his employer to move from Truro to Manchester.

The maximum amount of relocation expenses that his employer can pay without a taxable benefit arising is:

£	

Task 4.22

In 2016/17 Dave earns £20,000 a year in his employment with BCD plc, and also receives dividend income of £6,300 from the company.

Tick to show the maximum pension contribution that Dave can make in 2016/17, on which he can obtain tax relief.

	✓
£3,600	
£20,000	
£26,300	
£27,000	

Task 4.23

Zara works for KJ Ltd. She incurs the following travelling expenses in 2016/17:

	£
Travel from her home in Preston to her workplace in Manchester	1,500
Travel to meet clients	300
Travel from her home in Preston to a temporary workplace in Birmingham (temporary period is 18 months)	1,800

Zara's qualifying travel expenses for 2016/17 are:

£	

Task 4.24

Tick to show how the payroll deduction scheme for occupational pensions works.

	✓
The employer deducts the contribution after calculating income tax under PAYE.	
The employer deducts basic rate tax from the contribution and the employee gets higher rate relief by extending the basic rate band in the tax computation.	
The employer deducts the contribution before calculating income tax under PAYE.	
The employer deducts basic rate tax from the contribution and there is no higher rate tax relief.	

Task 4.25

Tick to show how tax relief is given on an employee's contribution to an occupational pension scheme.

	✓
The pension contribution is paid net of basic rate tax, and higher rate tax relief is obtained by extending the basic rate band.	
The contribution is deducted from employment income as an allowable expense before tax is calculated under PAYE.	

Task 4.26

This style of task is human marked in the live assessment.

You have received the following email from your client Martin Wilkes:

From: MartinWilkes@boxmail.net
To: AATStudent@boxmail.net
Sent: 12 March 2017 10:24
Subject: Car

I have just received a promotion, and my employer is offering me a company car for business and personal use from 6 April 2017. My employer is getting a good deal on the car because I looked up the list price, which is £18,000, but they are only paying £14,000 after a discount from the dealer. I also noted that the car has CO_2 emissions of 173 g/km.

My employer will pay all the running costs of the car and will also provide all the fuel. I will pay £20 a month towards private fuel, but I think that my actual private fuel used would cost about £50.

Can you please explain all of the taxation aspects of the provision of this car as a taxable benefit? Is there any other information that you need to know?

Thanks,

Martin Wilkes

Reply to Martin's email, explaining to him the various taxation aspects that can apply to the provision of the car. Assume rates stay unchanged for future years.

From: AATStudent@boxmail.net
To: MartinWilkes@boxmail.net
Sent: 14 March 2017 12:29
Subject: Car

Chapter 5 – Property income

Task 5.1

Simran rents out a furnished house from 1 July 2016. The rent is £500 per month, payable on the first day of each month. She incurs the following costs relating to the rental:

	£
Electricity for 1 July 2016 to 31 March 2017	1,200
Water rates for 1 July 2016 to 31 March 2017	500
Insurance for 1 July 2016 to 30 June 2017	360
Replacement furniture purchased on 1 August 2016	400

Tick to show what Simran's property income for 2016/17 is.

	✓
£2,080	
£1,990	
£2,040	
£2,130	

Task 5.2

Julie received the following property income during 2016/17:

(1) Annual rental of £6,300 (payable in advance) from a furnished flat first let on 6 August 2016. During the tax year the Julie spent £420 on replacement furniture and allowable expenses of £660. The tenant is responsible for paying water rates and council tax.

(2) £3,500 from renting out her garage in London for parking.

What amount of taxable property income does Julie have for 2016/17?

£	

Task 5.3

Zelda lets out a house. Her accrued income and allowable expenses are as follows:

	Income £	Expenses £
2014/15	6,000	10,000
2015/16	8,000	5,500
2016/17	10,000	4,000

Zelda's property income for 2016/17 is:

£	

Task 5.4

On 1 October 2016 Nitin buys a badly dilapidated house for £350,000. During October 2016, he spends £40,000 on making the house habitable. He lets it furnished for £3,600 a month from 1 November 2016, but the tenant leaves on 31 January 2017. A new tenant moves in on 1 March 2017, paying £4,000 a month rent.

Water rates are £195 for the period 1 October 2016 to 31 March 2017, payable by Nitin. He also pays buildings insurance of £480 for the period from 1 October 2016 to 30 September 2017. He financed the purchase of £350,000 with a bank loan at 5% interest. He spends £1,461 on replacement carpets in February 2017.

Nitin's property income for 2016/17 is:

£	

Task 5.5

Sinead starts to let out property on 1 July 2016.

(1) On 1 July 2016, she lets a house which she has owned for several years. The tenant is required to pay annual rent of £8,000, quarterly in advance. The house is let unfurnished. She incurs total allowable expenses of £1,200 in relation to this letting.

(2) On 1 December 2016, she lets out a house which she has bought. The tenant pays rent of £450 per month, payable on the first of each month. The house is let unfurnished. She incurs total allowable expenses of £2,000 in relation to this letting.

Sinead's property income for 2016/17 is:

£	

Task 5.6

In 2016/17, Sally makes a property income loss of £(5,000) on letting out Red Roofs, and property income profit of £3,000 on letting out Green Acres. Sally also has employment income of £20,000 in 2016/17.

Sally can obtain loss relief by: (tick ONE box)

	✓
Setting the loss of £(5,000) against her employment income in 2016/17	
Carrying forward the loss of £(5,000) against property income in 2017/18	
Setting the loss of £(5,000) first against the profit of £3,000 in 2016/17 and then carrying forward the balance of £(2,000) against property income in 2017/18	
Setting the loss of £(5,000) first against the profit of £3,000 in 2016/17 and then setting the balance of £(2,000) against employment income in 2016/17	

Task 5.7

Pierce Jones owns a flat that he rents out for £500 per calendar month, payable on the first day of each month. The property is let unfurnished. His other expenses for 2016/17 were:

	£
Electricity and gas	1,200
Water rates	400
Purchase of a television (not a replacement)	1,200
Mortgage interest	3,200
Insurance	250

What is his assessable property income for 2016/17?

£	

Task 5.8

(a) Property income is assessed as: (tick ONE box)

	✓
Non-savings income	
Savings income	
Dividend income	
Not taxable	

(b) Property income is taxed at: (tick ONE box)

	✓
20/40/45%	
10/20/40/45%	
0/7.5/32.5/38.1%	
0/20/40/45%	

Chapter 6 – Taxable income

Task 6.1

For each of the following sources of income, indicate whether it is non-savings income, savings income or dividend income by ticking the relevant box:

	Non-savings income	Savings income	Dividend income
Trading income			
Dividend received from a company			
Property income			
Building society interest			
Bank interest			
Pension income			
Employment income			
Interest from government stock ('gilts')			

Task 6.2

Olive received the following income in 2016/17.

Show the amount of income that she should enter on her tax return. If the income is exempt, enter 0.

(a) Bank account interest £160

£	

(b) Premium bond prize £100

£	

(c) Dividends £540

£	

Task 6.3

For each of the following interest payments, indicate whether they are received gross, net of basic rate tax or are exempt from income tax by ticking the relevant box:

	Gross	Net	Exempt
Bank interest			
Interest on an individual savings account (ISA)			
Building society interest			
Interest from government stock ('gilts')			

Task 6.4

You act for Jonty, who was born in July 1969. The following information is relevant for the year ended 5 April 2017:

(1) His salary was £38,730.

(2) His other income received was:

	£
Building society interest	80
Dividends	63

Jonty's taxable income for 2016/17 is:

£	

Task 6.5

Mr Betteredge has the following income for 2016/17:

	£
Salary for the year to 5 April 2017	15,665
Interest received (amount received shown):	
National Westminster Bank plc	457
ISA account	180
Nationwide Building Society account	400

Using the proforma layout provided, prepare a schedule of income for 2016/17, clearly showing the distinction between non-savings and savings income. If income is exempt, enter 0. Mr Betteredge's personal allowance should be deducted as appropriate. Fill in ALL the unshaded boxes, and add a 0 (zero) if necessary.

	Non-savings income £	Savings income £	Total £
Earnings			
Bank deposit interest			
Building society interest			
ISA interest			
Net income			
Less personal allowance			
Taxable income			

Task 6.6

Hayley receives employment income of £95,000, bank interest of £1,600, ISA interest of £2,000 and dividends of £4,500 in 2016/17.

(a) Hayley's net income for 2016/17 is:

£	

(b) The personal allowance that Hayley is entitled to for 2016/17 is:

£	

Task 6.7

Max has net income of £116,000 for 2016/17. He made Gift Aid donations of £4,000 (gross) during the year.

Max's personal allowance for 2016/17 is:

£	

Task 6.8

Gavin was born in September 1932. In 2016/17, he receives pension income of £19,300, bank interest of £2,000, dividends of £5,400 and lottery winnings of £6,000.

(a) Gavin's net income for 2016/17 is:

£	

(b) The personal allowance that Gavin is entitled to for 2016/17 is:

£	

Task 6.9

From 6 April 2016 the maximum an individual can invest for the tax year in an ISA is:

£	

Task 6.10

Tick to show whether the following statement is True or False.

Scholarships and educational grants are exempt as income of the student.

	✓
True	
False	

Task 6.11

Tick to show whether the following statement is True or False.

Damages received for an injury at work are only sometimes exempt from income tax, whereas damages paid on death are always exempt from income tax.

	✓
True	
False	

Chapter 7 – Calculation of income tax

Task 7.1

Guy receives bank interest of £7,500 in 2016/17.

Calculate the income tax liability assuming he has non savings income before PA of:

(a) £12,000 (show whole pounds only)

£	

(b) £41,000 (show whole pounds only)

£	

Task 7.2

You act for Deidre Watkins. Deidre was born in 1959 and has the following taxable income for 2016/17:

Non-savings income	£14,700
Savings income	£2,176
Dividend income	£1,766

Calculate Deidre's tax liability (show whole pounds only) on each source of income for 2016/17 as follows:

(a) Non-savings income:

£	

(b) Savings income:

£	

(c) Dividend income:

£	

Task 7.3

Peter has non-savings income of £205,000 and makes a personal pension contribution of £12,000 in December 2016.

Tick to show the amount of Peter's additional rate threshold in 2016/17.

	✓
£150,000	
£162,000	
£165,000	
£155,000	

Task 7.4

Tony is a higher rate taxpayer and makes a Gift Aid donation of £6,000 in December 2016.

Tick to show the amount of Tony's basic rate band in 2016/17.

	✓
£38,000	
£32,000	
£39,500	
£38,667	

Task 7.5

Katy is an additional rate taxpayer and makes a Gift Aid donation of £4,000 in June 2016.

(a) Katy's basic rate band for 2016/17 is:

£	

(b) Katy's higher rate band for 2016/17 is:

£	

(c) Katy's additional rate threshold for 2016/17 is:

£	

Task 7.6

Ruth has non-savings income of £30,000, savings income of £2,000 and dividend income of £6,000.

(a) Ruth's personal savings allowance for 2016/17 is:

£	

(b) Ruth's dividend allowance for 2016/17 is:

£	

Task 7.7

Rachel (born in 1966) received £23,500 bank interest in 2016/17. This is her only income.

Rachel's income tax liability for 2016/17 is:

£	

Task 7.8

Richard has taxable non-savings income of £58,525 in 2016/17. He made pension contributions to his personal pension scheme of £10,800 during the year. Tax of £9,700 was deducted under the PAYE system.

Richard's income tax payable for 2016/17 is:

£	

Task 7.9

John Smith has the following income and outgoings for the tax year 2016/17:

	£
Salary (£8,500 tax deducted under PAYE)	50,000
Interest on a deposit account with the Scotia Bank	800
Donation under the Gift Aid scheme made on 1 September 2016	2,400
Dividends received on UK shares	1,000

(a) Using the proforma layout provided, prepare a schedule of income for 2016/17, clearly showing the distinction between non-savings, savings and dividend income. Fill in all the unshaded boxes. If an answer is zero input 0.

	Non-savings income £	Savings income £	Dividend income £	Total £
Salary				
Dividend				
Bank deposit interest				
Net income				
Less personal allowance				
Taxable income				

(b) John's income tax liability for 2016/17 is:

£	

(c) John's income tax payable for 2016/17 is:

£	

Task 7.10

Jean Brown has the following income and outgoings for the tax year 2016/17:

	£
Salary (£48,500 tax deducted under PAYE)	155,000
Interest on a bank deposit account	3,000
Personal pension contribution	8,000
Dividends received on UK shares	10,000

(a) Using the proforma layout provided, prepare a schedule of income for 2016/17, clearly showing the distinction between non-savings, savings and dividend income. Fill in all the unshaded boxes. If an answer is zero input 0.

	Non-savings income £	Savings income £	Dividend income £	Total £
Salary				
Dividend				
Bank deposit interest				
Net income				
Less personal allowance				
Taxable income				

(b) Jean's income tax liability for 2016/17 is:

£	

(c) Jean's income tax payable for 2016/17 is:

£	

Task 7.11

This style of task is human marked in the live assessment.

During 2016/17 Joshua, who was born in 1940, has income as follows:

Pension income	£9,200
Bank interest received	£11,075
Dividends received	£10,000

Joshua made a Gift Aid donation of £1,500 in July 2016.

Calculate Joshua's total income tax liability for 2016/17, using the table given below. Show your answer in whole pounds.

Task 7.12

This style of task is human marked in the live assessment.

During 2016/17 Jack has income as follows:

Trading income	£90,000
Bank interest received	£1,500
Dividends received	£15,000

Calculate Jack's total income tax liability for 2016/17, using the table given below. Show your answer in whole pounds.

				£

Chapter 8 – Chargeable gains

Task 8.1

Fill in the boxes.

For the gain on the disposal of a capital asset to be a chargeable gain there must be a chargeable

of a chargeable

by a chargeable

Task 8.2

Tick to show whether the following assets are chargeable assets or exempt assets for capital gains tax.

Item	Chargeable asset	Exempt asset
Car		
A plot of land		
Jewellery		
Premium bonds		
Government stock ('gilts')		

Task 8.3

Tick to show which ONE of the following is not a chargeable disposal for capital gains purposes.

	✓
The gift of an asset	
The sale of part of an asset	
The transfer of an asset on death	
The sale of the whole of an asset	

Task 8.4

Kate purchased a freehold property for £40,000. Kate then spent £5,000 on a new roof for the property as the old roof was storm damaged prior to acquisition. She sold the property for £90,100 on 15 March 2017. Kate had not made any other disposals during 2016/17.

What is Kate's taxable gain for 2016/17?

	✓
£34,000	
£39,000	
£45,000	
£50,000	

Task 8.5

In November 2016, Lenny made chargeable gains of £20,100 and allowable losses of £3,560. He made no other disposals during 2016/17 and is a higher rate taxpayer.

(a) Lenny's capital gains tax liability for 2016/17 is:

£	

(b) Lenny's capital gains tax liability is payable by: (insert date as xx/xx/xxxx)

Task 8.6

In November 2016, Larry made chargeable gains of £25,100 and allowable losses of £5,200. He made no other disposals during 2016/17. He has £4,000 of his basic rate tax band remaining.

Larry's capital gains tax liability for 2016/17 is:

£	

Task 8.7

Laura made chargeable gains of £5,100 in July 2016 and £17,500 in November 2016. In May 2016 she made allowable losses of £2,000. Laura has taxable income of £29,935 for 2016/17.

Laura's capital gains tax liability for 2016/17 is:

£	

Task 8.8

Lisa made chargeable gains of £27,100 in December 2016. She made no other disposals in the year. Her taxable income for 2016/17 was £26,035.

Lisa's capital gains tax liability for 2016/17 is:

£	

Task 8.9

Darren bought a 3 acre plot of land for £150,000. He sold two acres of the land at auction for £240,000. His disposal costs were £3,000. The market value of the one remaining acre at the date of sale was £60,000.

(a) The cost of the land sold is:

£	

(b) The chargeable gain on sale is:

£	

Task 8.10

Tick to show how a taxpayer will pay the capital gains tax due for 2016/17.

	✓
The full amount will be paid on 31 January 2018	
The full amount will be paid on 31 January 2017	
Payments on account will be made on 31 January and 31 July 2017, with the balance being paid on 31 January 2018	
Payments on account will be made on 31 January and 31 July 2016, with the balance being paid on 31 January 2017	

Task 8.11

Mattheus made gains of £18,200 and losses of £7,000 in 2016/17. He has losses brought forward of £5,000.

The losses to carry forward to 2017/18 are (do not use brackets or a minus sign):

£	

Task 8.12

Mike inherited a valuable painting from a distant uncle in November 2008. The painting had cost his uncle £5,000 in January 2001 and was valued at £9,000 at the date of his death. Luckily for Mike, when he sold it in December 2016, the proceeds were £16,000.

Mike's chargeable gain on sale is:

£	

Task 8.13

Luke sells one acre of land in August 2016 for £25,000. His disposal costs were £2,500. He had bought four acres of land for £15,000. The market value of the remaining land was £50,000 at the date of sale. The acquisition costs of the four acres of land were £1,500.

Luke's chargeable gain on sale is:

£	

Task 8.14

Tick to show whether the following statement is True or False.

If an individual has allowable losses brought forward, these are only used to bring gains down to the annual exempt amount.

	✓
True	
False	

Task 8.15

James has the following gains and losses arising from disposals of chargeable assets:

Tax year	2014/15	2015/16	2016/17
Gains	£2,000	£4,000	£13,400
Losses	£(14,000)	£(2,000)	£(2,000)

The maximum allowable loss carried forward to 2017/18 will be:

£	

Task 8.16

Mary is married to Mike. They have a daughter, Beatrice. Mike has a sister, Susan who is married to Simon. Susan and Simon have a daughter called Sarah.

Tick which ONE of the following is not a connected person in relation to Mary.

	✓
Beatrice	
Susan	
Simon	
Sarah	

Task 8.17

Joanne gives an asset to her son in September 2016. There was an allowable loss on the disposal of £(3,000). Joanne also gave an asset to her daughter in October 2016. There was a chargeable gain of £5,000 on this disposal.

Tick to show whether the following statement is True or False.

The loss of £(3,000) can be set against the gain of £5,000.

	✓
True	
False	

Task 8.18

Xena bought a vase for £1,500 and sold it in October 2016 for £6,500, incurring expenses of sale of £130.

Her chargeable gain on sale is:

£	

Task 8.19

Jolyon purchased a gold ring for £7,000. He sold it in January 2017 for £3,000. The expenses of sale were £125.

Jolyon's allowable loss is (do not use brackets or a minus sign):

£	

Task 8.20

Rowenna bought a necklace for £4,000. She sold it in September 2016 for £5,500.

Tick to show whether the following statement is True or False.

Rowenna has a chargeable gain on sale of £1,500.

	✓
True	
False	

Task 8.21

Gilda purchased a picture for £3,500 and sold it in September 2016 for £7,500, incurring £300 expenses of sale.

Tick to show the chargeable gain on sale of the picture.

	✓
£1,200	
£2,000	
£2,500	
£3,700	

Task 8.22

Mark purchased an antique vase for £9,000. He sold the vase in August 2016 at auction for £4,500 net of auctioneer's fees of £500.

Mark's allowable loss is (both minus signs and brackets can be used to indicate negative numbers):

£	

Chapter 9 – Share disposals

Task 9.1

On 17 January 2017 Lionel sold 10,000 ordinary shares in Old plc. He had originally purchased 12,000 shares in Old plc on 10 May 2008, and purchased another 8,000 shares on 24 January 2017.

Tick to show how Lionel's disposal of 10,000 shares in Old plc will be matched with his acquisitions.

	✓
Against 10,000 of the shares purchased on 10 May 2008	
Against 5,000 of the shares purchased on 24 January 2017 and then against 5,000 of the shares purchased on 10 May 2008	
Against 10,000 of the total shareholding of 20,000 shares	
Against the 8,000 shares purchased on 24 January 2017 and then against 2,000 of the shares purchased on 10 May 2008	

Task 9.2

Mr Stevens sold 5,000 ordinary shares in JKL plc for £20,000 on 10 August 2016. He bought 6,000 shares in JKL plc for £9,000 on 15 July 2015 and another 1,000 shares for £4,200 on 16 August 2016.

His net chargeable gain on sale is:

£	

Task 9.3

This style of task is human marked in the live assessment.

Eloise's dealings in Moo plc were as follows:

	No. of shares	Cost/proceeds £
10 February 2001	12,000	18,000
20 September 2008	Bonus issue of 1 for 4	Nil
15 March 2017	(2,000)	8,000

Using the proforma layout provided, calculate Eloise's gain on sale. Fill in all the unshaded boxes and if the answer is zero insert '0'. Both minus signs and brackets can be used to indicate negative numbers.

Share pool

	No. of shares	Cost £
10 February 2001		
20 September 2008 Bonus 1:4		
15 March 2017 Disposal		

Gain on sale

	£
Proceeds	
Less cost	
Gain	

Task 9.4

This style of task is human marked in the live assessment.

Mark sold 10,000 of his shares in AC plc on 4 November 2016 for £60,000. The shares had been acquired as follows:

	No. of shares	Cost £
9 December 2001	12,000	4,400
12 October 2005 (Rights issue 1:3 at £5)		
10 November 2016	2,000	11,500

Calculate Mark's total chargeable gain on sale. All workings must be shown. If the answer is zero insert '0'. Both minus signs and brackets can be used to indicate negative numbers.

Task 9.5

This style of task is human marked in the live assessment.

Darren sold 700,000 of his shares in R plc on 24 September 2016 for £3,675,000. The shares had been acquired as follows:

	No. of shares	Cost £
2 June 2006	500,000	960,000
1 December 2011 (Bonus issue 3:2)		

Calculate Darren's total chargeable gain on sale. All workings must be shown. If the answer is zero insert '0'. Both minus signs and brackets can be used to indicate negative numbers.

Chapter 10 – Principal private residence

Task 10.1

Nicole is selling her main residence, which she has owned for 25 years. She lived in the house for the first eight years of ownership, let the property for the next five years whilst she was posted abroad by her employer, returned to live in the house for the next two years, and then moved out for the remainder of her period of ownership.

Tick to show what fraction of her gain will be exempt under the private residence exemption.

	✓
16.5/25	
8.5/25	
15.5/25	
11.5/25	

Task 10.2

Mr Kitch bought a house in 2005 and lived in it until December 2015 when he moved out to live with his girlfriend. He sold the house in December 2016 and made a gain of £30,000.

The whole gain will be covered by PPR relief.

	✓
True	
False	

Task 10.3

Mr Fox bought a house on 1 August 1998 for £50,000. He lived in the house until 31 July 2001. He then went abroad to work as a self-employed engineer until 31 July 2006. He lived in the house again until 31 January 2007, when he moved out.

Mr Fox sold the house on 31 July 2016 for £180,000.

Using the proforma layout provided, calculate the chargeable gain on sale.

	£
Proceeds	
Less cost	
Gain before PPR exemption	
Less PPR exemption	
Chargeable gain	

Task 10.4

Jose purchased a house and lived in it for three years. The house was then unoccupied for five years when he was required to work abroad in Spain. He moved back to the UK and lived in the house for two years before moving out to live with his girlfriend. The house was unoccupied for four years before he moved back to the house for the final year of ownership.

Tick to show what fraction of his gain will be exempt under the private residence exemption.

	✓
14.5/15	
14/15	
13.5/15	
15/15	

Task 10.5

David purchased a house in 2003. He lived in the property for a year before going travelling for four years. He moved back to the property for five years before going to work abroad for his current employer. He sold the house in 2016 without returning to the property.

All periods of absence will be covered by PPR relief.

	✓
True	
False	

Answer Bank

Chapter 1

Task 1.1

The tax year 2016/17 runs from:

06/04/2016

until:

05/04/2017

Task 1.2

	✓
True	✓
False	

Task 1.3

The UK tax system is administered by.

	✓
Parliament	
Her Majesty's Revenue & Customs (HMRC)	✓
National Crime Agency (NCA)	
HM Customs & Excise	

Task 1.4

	✓
HMRC	
Your firm's Money Laundering Reporting Officer	✓
National Crime Agency	
Tax Tribunal	

Task 1.5

Please be assured that an ethical guideline of confidentiality applies in your dealings with our firm. This guideline means that your personal information will remain confidential, unless you give us authority to disclose information to third parties such as members of your family.

Task 1.6

	✓
If the client is unwell and unable to respond to HMRC	
If money laundering is suspected	✓
Where it would be illegal not to disclose the information	✓
If the information is requested from a 'connected person'	

Task 1.7

The five fundamental principles of professional ethics for AAT members are:

I	Integrity
O	Objectivity
Pc and dc	Professional competence and due care
C	Confidentiality
Pb	Professional behaviour

Task 1.8

	✓
HMRC	
Another firm's Money Laundering Reporting Officer	
National Crime Agency	✓
Tax Tribunal	

Task 1.9

	✓
True	
False	✓

A non-UK resident individual is only liable to pay income tax on their UK income.

Task 1.10

You should inform the client that this represents theft and they should tell HMRC of their mistake immediately.

If they refuse to tell HMRC then you will need to warn them of the consequences of not informing HMRC of their mistake. If HMRC do discover this error then there would be interest and penalties (criminal and civil) due as well as the expectation that the initial amount of the refund would need to be repaid.

If they still refuse then you should cease to act for the client and inform HMRC that you have ceased to act for them. You cannot tell HMRC why you are ceasing to act for the client as this would be a breach of confidentiality.

You have a professional responsibility to neither break the law nor assist others to do so.

Ensure all correspondence is in writing and saved in the file.

Task 1.11

	✓
True	
False	✓

Tax avoidance is the use of tax legislation in a way that was not intended to reduce tax liabilities. It is legal but can be considered unethical.

Tax evasion is illegal.

Chapter 2

Task 2.1

	Class 1 Primary	Class 1 Secondary	Class 1A	None
Salary	✓	✓		
Company car			✓	
Mileage expenses paid at 35p per mile				✓
Bonus	✓	✓		
Department store vouchers	✓	✓		
Reimbursed travel expenses				✓
Private gym membership			✓	

Task 2.2

(a) Class 1 Primary

£	2,445

(b) Class 1 Secondary

£	2,882

(c) Class 1A

£	414

Workings:

£27,000/12 months = £2,250 per month.

Primary		£
£(2,250 – 672) = 1,578 × 12% × 11 months	=	2,083
£(3,583 – 672) = 2,911 × 12% × 1 month	=	349
£(2,250 + £2,000 – 3,583) = 667 × 2% × 1 month	=	13
	=	2,445

Secondary		£
£(2,250 – 676) = 1,574 × 13.8% × 11 months	=	2,389
£(2,250 +2,000 – 676) × 13.8% × 1 month	=	493
	=	2,882
1A		
£3,000 × 13.8%	=	414

Task 2.3

	✓
Class 1 Primary on £45,300 and Class 1A on £300	
Class 1 Primary and Secondary on £45,000 and Class 1A on £300	✓
Class 1 Primary and Secondary on £45,300	
Class 1 Primary and Secondary on £45,300 and Class 1A on £300	

Task 2.4

	✓
True	
False	✓

False: this is above the statutory maximum of 45p per mile and so Class 1 primary and secondary would be payable on the excess.

Task 2.5

	✓
True	
False	✓

False: vouchers are deemed to be cash equivalents and so Class 1 Primary and Secondary contributions would be due on the cash amount of the vouchers.

Task 2.6

	✓
£987	
£5,106	
£3,987	✓
£2,106	

Workings: £(37,000 – 8,112) × 13.8% = £3,987. The employment allowance is not available as Freya is the sole employed earner and a director of Wise Ltd.

Task 2.7

What national insurance contributions are payable by employers and employees on a company car benefit? Please choose from the picklist below:

Employers	Class 1A
Employees	None

Employees do not pay national insurance on benefits.

Chapter 3

Task 3.1

	PET	CLT	Exempt
Gift of £100 cash to niece			✓ small gift
Gift of shares to a trust		✓	
Payment of grandson's school fees out of income surplus to living requirements			✓ Payment out of income – does not reduce standard of living
Gift of £5,000 to son on the occasion of his marriage			✓
Gift of £25,000 to friend	✓		
Gift of classic car to spouse			✓ Transfers between spouses/civil partners are exempt
Gift of £10,000 to a trust		✓	

Task 3.2

£	550,000

Norman's nil band at death was £325,000 with £100,000 being used on the transfer to his cousin. The remaining £225,000 is added to the nil band of Maureen of £325,000 making a total nil band of £550,000 available to Maureen on her death.

Task 3.3

	Deductible ✓	Not deductible ✓
Grocery bill	✓	
HM Revenue & Customs – income tax to death	✓	
Mortgage on home	✓	
Illegal gambling debt		✓

Grocery bill – deductible as incurred for consideration

Income tax to death – deductible as imposed by law

Mortgage – deductible, will be set against value of house primarily

Illegal gambling debt – not deductible as not legally enforceable

Task 3.4

	✓
True	
False	✓

A PET is only subject to Inheritance Tax on the death of the donor if the death occurs within seven years of the gift

Task 3.5

	✓
True	
False	✓

The £5,000 exemption only applies to gifts on marriage from parent to child.

Task 3.6

Lifetime tax	Death tax	✓
31 January 2017	30 June 2017	
30 April 2017	30 June 2017	✓
31 January 2017	30 April 2017	
30 April 2017	30 April 2017	

Lifetime tax 30 April 2017, death tax 30 June 2017

For chargeable lifetime transfers the due date is the later of 30 April just after the end of the tax year of the transfer and six months after the end of the month of the transfer. The due date for the tax arising on death is six months from the end of the month of death.

Task 3.7

	✓
£87,250	✓
£69,800	
£88,750	
£22,500	

Workings:

	£
Gift	420,000
Less AEs 2016/17, 2015/16 b/f	(6,000)
Net chargeable transfer	414,000
Less nil band remaining £(325,000 – 260,000)	(65,000)
	349,000
IHT @ 20/80	87,250

The gross chargeable transfer in August 2012 is after any exemptions but the gift in November 2016 must have the annual exemptions deducted to find the net chargeable transfer.

Task 3.8

257.5	**p**

Workings: lower of:

$\frac{1}{4}$ up: $\frac{280 - 250}{4} + 250 = 257.5$

Average: $\frac{279 - 252}{2} = 265.5$

Task 3.9

£	2,750

Workings:

	£
Before transfer: 500 shares at £10	5,000
After transfer: 300 shares at £7.50	2,250
Transfer of value	2,750

Chapter 4

Task 4.1

	✓
True	
False	✓

An employee has a contract of service.

Task 4.2

Factor	Contract of service	Contract for services
Peter is entitled to paid holidays	✓	
Peter hires his own helpers		✓
Peter takes substantial financial risks when undertaking work for XYZ plc		✓
Peter does not have to rectify mistakes in his work at his own expense	✓	

Task 4.3

Item	£
Salary	24,280
Commission	0
Employer's pension contribution	0
Bonus	1,200

Salary paid on the first of each month, therefore received in 2016/17 as follows:

1 May 2016 to 1 September 2016 = 5 × £2,000 = £10,000

1 October 2016 to 1 April 2017 = 7 × £2,000 × 102% = £14,280

Salary = £10,000 + £14,280 = £24,280

Task 4.4

	✓
True	
False	✓

Tips received by a tour guide from customers are earnings. Note that earnings can include money received other than from the employer.

Task 4.5

The date of receipt of the bonus for employment income purposes is:

20/12/2016

Task 4.6

(a) The cost of the car in the taxable benefit computation is:

£	15,000

(b) The percentage used in the taxable benefit computation is:

32	%

The CO_2 emissions of the car are 176g/km (rounded down to the nearest five).

Amount over baseline figure: 175 – 95 = 80 g/km

Divide 80 by 5 = 16

The taxable percentage is 16% + 16% = 32%

(c) The taxable benefit on the provision of the car is:

£	3,200

32% × £15,000 × 8/12 (6 August 2016 to 5 April 2017)

Task 4.7

(a) The taxable benefit on the provision of the car is:

£	5,900

Round down CO_2 emissions to 150 g/km

Amount above baseline: 150 – 95 = 55 g/km

Divide 55 by 5 = 11

Taxable % = 16% + 11% + 3% (diesel) = 30%

	£
£25,000 × 30% × 10/12	6,250
Less employee contribution (10 × £35)	(350)
Taxable benefit of car	5,900

(b) The taxable benefit on the provision of fuel is:

£	5,550

£22,200 × 30% × 10/12 = £5,550

Task 4.8

(a) The cost of the car in the taxable benefit computation is:

£	11,500

(b) The percentage used in the taxable benefit computation is:

14	%

As CO_2 emissions are from 51g to 75g/km = 11% + 3% (diesel)

(c) The taxable benefit in respect of the provision of fuel for private use is:

£	3,108

£22,200 × 14%

Task 4.9

(a) The percentage used in the taxable benefit computation is:

	✓
22	
37	✓
38	
41	

Round down CO_2 emissions to 205 g/km

Amount above baseline: 205 – 95 = 110 g/km

Divide 110 by 5 = 22

Taxable % = 16% + 22% + 3% (diesel) = 41%, max 37%

(b) The taxable benefit in respect of the provision of the car is:

£	19,240

	£
List price	57,000
Less capital contribution paid by employee (max)	(5,000)
Cost of car	52,000
Car benefit £52,000 × 37%	19,240

(c) The taxable benefit in respect of the provision of fuel for private use is:

£	8,214

£22,200 × 37% = £8,214 There is no reduction for part reimbursement of private fuel.

Task 4.10

	✓
£3,170	
£3,768	
£598	
Nil	✓

There is no taxable benefit because there is no private use of the van – travel from home to work is not private use for vans.

Task 4.11

The taxable benefit for 2016/17 is:

£	110

The benefit taxable in 2015/16 was 20% × £200 = £40

The benefit taxable in 2016/17 will be the greater of:

		£	£
(1)	Market value at acquisition by employee	120	
(2)	Original market value	200	
	Less benefit for use in 2015/16	(40)	
		160	
	Ie		160
	Less price paid by employee		(50)
	Taxable benefit 2016/17		110

Task 4.12

(a) Using the average method, the taxable benefit for 2016/17 is:

£	50

	£
3% × (50,000 + 20,000)/2	1,050
Less interest paid	(1,000)
Taxable benefit	50

(b) Using the alternative method, the taxable benefit for 2016/17 is:

£	200

	£
£50,000 × 8/12 × 3%	1,000
(6 April 2016 to 5 December 2016)	
£20,000 × 4/12 × 3%	200
(6 December 2016 to 5 April 2017)	
	1,200
Less interest paid	(1,000)
Taxable benefit	200

Task 4.13

	✓
True	
False	✓

There is a taxable benefit of the amount of the loan written-off, however small the loan. The £10,000 limit only applies to the interest benefit.

Task 4.14

(a) The taxable benefit for 2016/17 is:

£	650

During 2016/17 Vimal will have a taxable benefit arising from the use of the asset:

£1,000 × 20% × 9/12 = £150

He will also have a benefit when the asset is sold to him at an undervalue.

This will be the higher of the MV at the date of the 'gift', and the original market value minus benefits assessed so far, less his £100 contribution.

	£	£
Market value at date of gift		300
Original market value		1,000
Assessed re use:		
2014/15: £1,000 × 20% × 3/12	50	
2015/16: £1,000 × 20%	200	
2016/17: £1,000 × 20% × 9/12	150	
		(400)
		600
ie Higher value used		600
Less Vimal's contribution		(100)
		500
His total benefit (for both use and 'gift') in 2016/17 will therefore be		650

(b) The taxable benefit for 2016/17 is:

£	4,350

The taxable benefit for use of the flat is calculated as follows:

	£
Annual value	3,000
£(120,000 – 75,000) × 3% (expensive accommodation)	1,350
Taxable benefit	4,350

The original cost is used, not the value now.

Task 4.15

The total taxable benefits for 2016/17 are:

£	625

	£
Medical insurance (cost to employer)	385
Childcare (exempt – £55 per week for a basic rate taxpayer)	0
Newspaper allowance (12 × £20)	240
Taxable benefits	625

Task 4.16

(a) The taxable benefit arising in respect of the accommodation provided for Rita in 2016/17 and purchase of the furniture is:

£	21,200

	£
Annual value (higher than rent paid)	4,000
Electricity	700
Gas	1,200
Water	500
Council tax	1,300
Repairs	3,500
Furniture (20% × £30,000 × 6/12)	3,000
Purchase of furniture (W)	7,000
	21,200

Working: Purchase of furniture

Benefit is the **higher** of:

		£
(1)	Cost	30,000
	Less taxed for use of furniture (20% × £30,000 × 6/12)	(3,000)
		27,000
	Less amount paid by Rita	(20,000)
		7,000
(2)	Market value	25,000
	Less amount paid	(20,000)
		5,000

(b) The taxable benefit arising in respect of the relocation expenses is:

£	4,000

£12,000 – £8,000

(c) The taxable benefit arising in respect of the interest free loan in 2016/17 is:

£	Nil

No taxable benefit arises if the combined outstanding balance on all loans to the employee did not exceed £10,000 at any time in the tax year.

Task 4.17

	✓
£800	
£1,460	
£260	✓
£660	

	£
Annual value	800
Less contribution (£100 × 12 = £1,200)	(800)
	Nil

Additional charge

	£	£
Cost	97,000	
Less	(75,000)	
Excess	22,000	
£22,000 × 3%		660
Less contribution (£1,200 – £800)		(400)
Total benefit 2016/17		260

Task 4.18

	✓
Taxable benefit of £700	
Allowable expense of £700	✓
Allowable expense of £1,300	
Taxable benefit of £4,550	

	£	£
Amount received 13,000 × 35p		4,550
Less statutory amounts		
10,000 × 45p	4,500	
3,000 × 25p	750	
		(5,250)
Allowable expense		(700)

Task 4.19

Item	Taxable	Exempt
Interest on loan of £2,000 (only loan provided)		✓
Removal costs of £6,000		✓
Use of pool car		✓
Reimbursement of business expenses		✓
One staff party costing £100 per head		✓
Accommodation provided to employee who is not required to live in it for the performance of employment	✓	
Provision of parking space at work		✓
Additional costs of home-working of £4 per week		✓
Long service award of £800 for 22 years service		✓
Accommodation provided to a caretaker for proper performance of his employment duties		✓
Work related training		✓
Provision of second mobile phone	✓	

Task 4.20

	£
Salary	30,000
Less allowable expenses:	
reimbursed expenses	0
pension contribution	(2,400)
professional body membership	(150)
fitness club membership	0
charitable donation	(600)
clothing	0
Employment income 2016/17	26,850

Task 4.21

The maximum amount of relocation expenses that his employer can pay without a taxable benefit arising is:

£	8,000

Task 4.22

	✓
£3,600	
£20,000	✓
£26,300	
£27,000	

The maximum contribution is the higher of £3,600 and his earnings of £20,000.

Dividends are not earnings.

Task 4.23

Zara's qualifying travel expenses for 2016/17 are:

£	2,100

£300 + £1,800. Travel expenses from home to a permanent workplace are not allowable.

Task 4.24

	✓
The employer deducts the contribution after calculating income tax under PAYE.	
The employer deducts basic rate tax from the contribution and the employee gets higher rate relief by extending the basic rate band in the tax computation.	
The employer deducts the contribution before calculating income tax under PAYE.	✓
The employer deducts basic rate tax from the contribution and there is no higher rate tax relief.	

The employer deducts the contribution before calculating income tax, so giving tax relief at the applicable rate/s.

Task 4.25

	✓
The pension contribution is paid net of basic rate tax, and higher rate tax relief is obtained by extending the basic rate band.	
The contribution is deducted from employment income as an allowable expense before tax is calculated under PAYE.	✓

Task 4.26

From: AATStudent@boxmail.net
To: MartinWilkes@boxmail.net
Sent: 14 March 2017 12:29
Subject: Car

The car benefit is a percentage of the car's list price, not the actual price paid by the employer.

The percentage (that is multiplied by the list price) is dependant on the car's C02 emissions rating. For cars which emit CO2 of 95g/km or more the percentage is 16%, however this percentage increases by 1% for every additional whole 5g/km of CO2 emissions above 95g/km, up to a maximum of 37%.

In this case, the percentage would be 16% + 15% = 31%.

The percentage is further increased by 3% for a diesel car – has this car got a petrol or a diesel engine?

As the employer will be paying for fuel used for private motoring, a fuel benefit arises. The benefit is a percentage of £22,200. The percentage is the same percentage as is used to calculate the car benefit, ie 31% in this instance.

No benefit arises if you reimburse the whole of the expense of any fuel provided for private use, but there is no reduction to the benefit if only part of the expense for private use fuel is reimbursed, as here. It would be better for the contribution to be set against the use of the car, as this would be deductible in calculating the car benefit.

Chapter 5

Task 5.1

Simran's property income for 2016/17 is:

	✓
£2,080	
£1,990	
£2,040	
£2,130	✓

	£
Rent received (9 months × £500 – accruals basis)	4,500
Less electricity	(1,200)
water rates	(500)
insurance 9/12 × £360	(270)
replacement furniture relief	(400)
Property income 2016/17	2,130

Task 5.2

The amount of taxable property income Julie has for 2016/17 is:

£	6,620

	£
Rent received (£6,300 × 8/12)	4,200
Less expenses	(660)
Replacement furniture relief	(420)
Garage	3,500
Property income 2016/17	6,620

Task 5.3

Zelda's property income for 2016/17 is:

£	4,500

	£
2014/15	
Income	6,000
Expenses	(10,000)
Loss cfwd	(4,000)
2015/16	
Income	8,000
Expenses	(5,500)
	2,500
Less loss b/f	(2,500)
	Nil
Loss cfwd £1,500 (£4,000 – £2,500)	
2016/17	
Income	10,000
Expenses	(4,000)
	6,000
Less loss b/f	(1,500)
Taxable property income 2016/17	4,500

Task 5.4

Nitin's property income for 2016/17 is:

£	4,154

	£
Rent (£3,600 × 3)	10,800
Rent (£4,000 × 1)	4,000
	14,800
Less water rates	(195)
insurance (£480 × 6/12)	(240)
interest (£350,000 × 5% × 6/12)	(8,750)
initial repairs: capital	0
replacement furniture relief	(1,461)
Property income 2016/17	4,154

Task 5.5

Sinead's property income for 2016/17 is:

£	4,600

	£
Property one: rent (9/12 × £8,000)	6,000
Property two: rent (4 × £450)	1,800
Less expenses on property one	(1,200)
expenses on property two	(2,000)
Property income 2016/17	4,600

Task 5.6

	✓
Setting the loss of £(5,000) against her employment income in 2016/17	
Carrying forward the loss of £(5,000) against property income in 2017/18	
Setting the loss of £(5,000) first against the profit of £3,000 in 2016/17 and then carrying forward the balance of £(2,000) against property income in 2017/18	✓
Setting the loss of £(5,000) first against the profit of £3,000 in 2016/17 and then setting the balance of £(2,000) against employment income in 2016/17	

Task 5.7

£	950

	£
Rent (£500 × 12)	6000
Rates and insurance(£400 + £250)	(650)
Mortgage interest	(3200)
Electricity and gas	(1200)
Property income 2016/17	950.00

The television is not a deductible expenses and does not qualify for replacement furniture relief.

Task 5.8

(a)

	✓
Non-savings income	✓
Savings income	
Dividend income	
Not taxable	

(b)

	✓
20/40/45%	✓
10/20/40/45%	
0/7.5/32.5/38.1%	
0/20/40/45%	

If the personal allowance is available to offset against some of the property income then that amount would not be taxable and the rest would be taxed at 20/40 and 45%.

Chapter 6

Task 6.1

	Non-savings income	Savings income	Dividend income
Trading income	✓		
Dividend received from a company			✓
Property income	✓		
Building society interest		✓	
Bank interest		✓	
Pension income	✓		
Employment income	✓		
Interest from government stock ('gilts')		✓	

Task 6.2

(a) Bank account interest £160

£	160

(b) Premium bond prize £100

£	0

Premium bond prizes are exempt income.

(c) Dividends £540

£	540

Task 6.3

	Gross	Net	Exempt
Bank interest	✓		
Interest on an individual savings account (ISA)			✓
Building society interest	✓		
Interest from government stock ('gilts')	✓		

Task 6.4

Jonty's taxable income for 2016/17 is:

£	27,873

	Non-savings income £	Savings income £	Dividend income £	Total £
Earnings	38,730			
Building society interest		80		
Dividends			63	
Net income	38,730	80	63	38,873
Less personal allowance	(11,000)			(11,000)
Taxable income	27,730	80	63	27,873

Task 6.5

	Non-savings income £	Savings income £	Total £
Earnings	15,665	0	
Bank deposit interest	0	457	
Building society interest	0	400	
ISA interest	0	0	
Net income	15,665	857	16,522
Less personal allowance	(11,000)	0	(11,000)
Taxable income	4,665	857	5,522

Task 6.6

(a) Hayley's net income for 2016/17 is:

£	102,000

	Non-savings income £	Savings income £	Dividend income £	Total £
Employment income	95,000			
Bank interest		1,600		
Dividends			4,500	
Net income	95,000	1,600	4,500	101,100

Note. ISA interest is exempt from income tax.

(b) The personal allowance that Hayley is entitled to for 2016/17 is:

£	10,450

	£
Net income	101,100
Less income limit	(100,000)
Excess	1,100
Personal allowance	11,000
Less half excess	(550)
	10,450

Task 6.7

Max's personal allowance for 2016/17 is:

£	5,000

	£
Net income	116,000
Less gift Aid donations (gross)	(4,000)
Adjusted net income	112,000
Less income limit	(100,000)
Excess	12,000
Personal allowance	11,000
Less half excess	(6,000)
	5,000

Task 6.8

(a) Gavin's net income for 2016/17 is:

£	26,700

	Non-savings income £	Savings income £	Dividend income £	Total £
Pension income	19,300			
Bank interest		2,000		
Dividends			5,400	
Net income	19,300	2,000	5,400	26,700

Note. Lottery winnings are exempt from income tax.

(b) The personal allowance that Gavin is entitled to for 2016/17 is:

£	11,000

Note. Personal age allowances have been abolished for 2016/17.

Task 6.9

From 6 April 2016 the maximum an individual can invest for the tax year in an ISA is:

£	15,240

Task 6.10

	✓
True	✓
False	

Task 6.11

The statement is false. Damages received for both injury and death are always exempt from income tax.

	✓
True	
False	✓

Chapter 7 Calculation of income tax

Task 7.1

(a) Guy's income tax liability is:

£	700

	Non-savings income £	**Savings income £**	**Total £**
Non-savings income	12,000		
Bank interest		7,500	
Net Income	12,000	7,500	19,500
PA	(11,000)		(11,000)
Taxable income	1,000	7,500	8,500
Tax:			
NSI £1,000 × 20%		200	
SI £5,000 – 1,000 = £4,000 × 0%		0	
SI £1,000 × 0% (PSA)		0	
SI £7,500 – 1,000 – 4,000 = £2,500 × 20%		500	
Income tax liability		700	

(b) Guy's income tax liability is:

£	8,500

	Non-savings income £	Savings income £	Total £
Non-savings income	41,000		
Interest		7,500	
Net income	41,000	7,500	47,500
PA	(11,000)		(11,000)
Taxable income	30,000	7,500	37,500
Tax:			
NSI £30,000 × 20%		6,000	
SI £500 × 0% (PSA: ANI > £43,000)		0	
SI £32,000 – 30,000 – 500 = £1,500 × 20%		300	
SI £7,500 – 500 – 1,500 = £5,500 × 40%		2,200	
Income tax liability		8,500	

Task 7.2

(a) Non-savings income:

£	2,940

(b) Savings income:

£	235

(c) Dividend income:

£	0

Note that 'taxable income' is the figure after the personal allowance.

	Non-savings income £	Savings income £	Dividend income £	Total £
Taxable income	14,700	2,176	1,766	18,642
Tax on non-savings income:	£14,700 × 20%		2,940	
Tax on savings income:				
£1,000 Basic Rate PSA	£1,000 × 0%		0	
Balance of Savings Income	£1,176 × 20%		235	
Tax on dividend income:				
Covered by £5,000 DA	£1,766 × 0%		0	
Income tax liability			3,175	

Task 7.3

	✓
£150,000	
£162,000	
£165,000	✓
£155,000	

Additional rate threshold £150,000 plus gross personal pension contribution of £15,000 (£12,000 × 100/80)

Task 7.4

	✓
£38,000	
£32,000	
£39,500	✓
£38,667	

Basic rate band extended by the gross Gift Aid donation, ie £(6,000 × 100/80) = £7,500

£32,000 + £7,500 = £39,500

Task 7.5

(a) Katy's basic rate band for 2016/17 is:

£	37,000

Basic rate band extended by the gross Gift Aid donation, ie £(4,000 × 100/80) = £5,000

£32,000 + £5,000

(b) Katy's higher rate band for 2016/17 is:

£	118,000

(£155,000 – £37,000)

(c) Katy's additional rate threshold for 2016/17 is:

£	155,000

Additional rate threshold = £37,000 + £118,000 (or £150,000 + £5,000)

Task 7.6

(a) Ruth's personal savings allowance for 2016/17 is:

£	1,000

Ruth is a basic rate taxpayer with ANI of <£43,000

(b) Ruth's dividend allowance for 2016/17 is:

£	5,000

The £5,000 dividend allowance is applicable to all taxpayers regardless of their marginal rate of tax.

Task 7.7

Rachel's income tax liability for 2016/17 is:

£	1,300

	£
Net income £23,500	23,500
Less personal allowance	(11,000)
Taxable income	12,500
£5,000 × 0% (starting rate)	0
£1,000 × 0% (PSA)	0
£12,500 – 5,000 – 1,000 = £6,500 × 20%	1,300
Income tax liability	1,300

Task 7.8

Richard's income tax payable for 2016/17 is:

£	4,610

'Taxable income' is the figure after personal allowances have been deducted

	£
Taxable income	58,525

		£
Tax	£32,000 × 20%	6,400
	£13,500 (extended by £10,800 × 100/80) × 20%	2,700
	£45,500	
	£13,025 × 40%	5,210
	£58,525	
Income tax liability		14,310
Less tax suffered at source (PAYE)		(9,700)
Income tax payable		4,610

Task 7.9

(a)

	Non-savings income £	Savings income £	Dividend income £	Total £
Salary	50,000	0	0	
Dividend	0	0	1,000	
Bank deposit interest	0	800	0	
Net income	50,000	800	1,000	51,800
Less personal allowance	(11,000)	0	0	(11,000)
Taxable income	39,000	800	1,000	40,800

The gross Gift Aid payment is £2,400 × 100/80 = £3,000.

The adjusted net income (51,800 – 3,000 Gift Aid) is in excess of £43,000 and so the £500 PSA applies.

(b) John's income tax liability for 2016/17 is:

£	8,720

(c) John's income tax payable for 2016/17 is:

£	220

	£
Tax on non-savings income	
£32,000 × 20%	6,400
£3,000 (extended band: Gift Aid £2,400 × 100/80) × 20%	600
£4,000 (£39,000 – 32,000 – 3,000) × 40%	1,600
Tax on savings income	
£500 × 0% (PSA)	0
£300 × 40%	120

	£
Tax on dividend income	
£1,000 × 0% (covered by DA)	0
Income tax liability	8,720
Less PAYE (given)	(8,500)
Income tax payable	220

Task 7.10

(a)

	Non-savings income £	Savings income £	Dividend income £	Total £
Salary	155,000	0	0	
Dividend	0	0	10,000	
Bank deposit interest	0	3,000	0	
Net income	155,000	3,000	10,000	168,000
Less personal allowance	0	0	0	0
Taxable income	155,000	3,000	10,000	168,000

The adjusted net income is in excess of £122,000 so the personal allowance is reduced to nil.

Additional rate tax payer and so the PSA does not apply.

(b) Jean's income tax liability for 2016/17 is:

£	56,705

(c) Jean's income tax payable for 2016/17 is:

£	8,205

	£
Tax on non-savings income	
£32,000 × 20%	6,400
£10,000 (extended band: pension) £8,000 × 100/80 × 20%	2,000
£113,000 × 40%	45,200
Tax on savings income	
£3,000 × 40%	1,200
Tax on dividend income	
£2,000 × 0% (DA)	0
£160,000 (extended higher rate band £150,000 + £10,000)	
£3,000 × 0% (DA £5,000 – £2,000)	0
£5,000 × 38.1%	1,905
Income tax liability	56,705

	£
Income tax liability b/fwd	56,705
Less tax deducted at source	
PAYE (given)	(48,500)
Income tax payable	8,205

Note. Additional rate threshold is increased by £10,000 to £160,000.

Task 7.11

	Non-savings income £	Savings income £	Dividend income £	Total £
Pension income	9,200			
Bank interest		11,075		
Dividends			10,000	
Net income	9,200	11,075	10,000	30,275
Personal allowance	(9,200)	(1,800)		(11,000)
Taxable income	Nil	9,275	10,000	19,275
Tax on savings income:				
£5,000 × 0%		0		
£1,000 × 0% (PSA)		0		
£3,275 (£9,275 – £6,000) × 20%		655		
Tax on dividend income:				
£5,000 × 0% (DA)		0		
£5,000 × 7.5%		375		
Income tax liability		1,030		

Adjusted net income ≤ £43,000 hence £1,000 PSA available.

Basic rate taxpayer therefore correct relief given at source so Gift Aid payment ignored.

Task 7.12

	Non-savings income £	Savings income £	Dividend income £	Total £
Trading income	90,000			
Bank interest		1,500		
Dividends			15,000	
Net income	90,000	1,500	15,000	106,500
Personal allowance (W)	(7,750)			(7,750)
Taxable income	82,250	1,500	15,000	98,750
Tax on non-savings income:				
£32,000 × 20%		6,400		
£50,250 × 40%		20,100		
Tax on savings income:				
£500 × 0% (PSA)		0		
£1,000 × 40%		400		
Tax on dividend income:				
£5,000 × 0% (DA)		0		
£10,000 × 32.5%		3,250		
Income tax liability		30,150		

(W) Jack has adjusted net income of £106,500 and therefore his personal allowance is restricted to: 11,000 – ((106,500 – 100,000) / 2) = £7,750.

Note. Jack is a higher rate tax payer and therefore only receives £500 PSA.

Chapter 8

Task 8.1

For the gain on the disposal of a capital asset to be a chargeable gain there must be a chargeable

disposal

of a chargeable

asset

by a chargeable

person

Task 8.2

Item	Chargeable asset	Exempt asset
Car		✓
A plot of land	✓	
Jewellery	✓	
Premium bonds		✓
Government stock ('gilts')		✓

Task 8.3

	✓
The gift of an asset	
The sale of part of an asset	
The transfer of an asset on death	✓
The sale of the whole of an asset	

Task 8.4

	✓
£34,000	✓
£39,000	
£45,000	
£50,000	

	£
Proceeds of sale	90,100
Less cost	(40,000)
Less enhancement expenditure	(5,000)
Chargeable gain	45,100
Less annual exempt amount	(11,100)
Taxable gain	34,000

Task 8.5

(a) Lenny's capital gains tax liability for 2016/17 is:

£	1,088

	£
Chargeable gains	20,100
Less allowable losses	(3,560)
Net chargeable gains	16,540
Less annual exempt amount	(11,100)
Taxable gains	5,440
CGT: £5,440 × 20%	1,088

(b) Lenny's capital gains tax liability is payable by:

31/01/2018

Task 8.6

Larry's capital gains tax liability for 2016/17 is:

£	1,360

	£
Chargeable gains	25,100
Less allowable losses	(5,200)
Net chargeable gains	19,900
Less annual exempt amount	(11,100)
Taxable gains	8,800

CGT payable

	£
£4,000 × 10%	400
£4,800 × 20%	960
	1,360

Task 8.7

Laura's capital gains tax liability for 2016/17 is:

£	1,694

	£
Chargeable gains (£5,100 + £17,500)	22,600
Less allowable losses	(2,000)
Net chargeable gains	20,600
Less annual exempt amount	(11,100)
Taxable gains	9,500

CGT payable

	£
£2,065 (W) × 10%	207
£7,435 × 20%	1,487
	1,694
(W) Unused basic rate band is £32,000 – £29,935 = £2,065	

Task 8.8

Lisa's capital gains tax liability for 2016/17 is:

£	2,604

	£
Chargeable gains	27,100
Less annual exempt amount	(11,100)
Taxable gains	16,000
CGT	
£5,965 (W) × 10%	597
£10,035 × 20%	2,007
	2,604
(W) Unused basic rate band is £32,000 – £26,035 = £5,965	

Task 8.9

(a) The cost of the land sold is:

£	120,000

$$\frac{240{,}000}{240{,}000 + 60{,}000} \times £150{,}000$$

(b) The chargeable gain on sale is:

£	117,000

	£
Disposal proceeds	240,000
Less disposal costs	(3,000)
Net proceeds	237,000
Less cost	(120,000)
Chargeable gain	117,000

Task 8.10

	✓
The full amount will be paid on 31 January 2018	✓
The full amount will be paid on 31 January 2017	
Payments on account will be made on 31 January and 31 July 2017, with the balance being paid on 31 January 2018	
Payments on account will be made on 31 January and 31 July 2016, with the balance being paid on 31 January 2017	

Task 8.11

The losses to carry forward to 2017/18 are:

£	4,900

	£
Gains	18,200
Losses	(7,000)
	11,200
Losses b/f £(11,200 – 11,100)	(100)
	11,100
Less annual exempt amount	(11,100)
Taxable gains	Nil

Losses c/f £(5,000 – 100) = £4,900

Task 8.12

Mike's chargeable gain on sale is:

£	7,000

	£
Proceeds of sale	16,000
Less allowable cost (value at death)	(9,000)
Chargeable gain	7,000

Task 8.13

Luke's chargeable gain on sale is:

£	17,000

	£
Proceeds of sale	25,000
Less disposal costs	(2,500)
Net proceeds of sale	22,500
Less allowable cost	
25,000/(25,000 + 50,000) × £(15,000 + 1,500)	(5,500)
Chargeable gain	17,000

Task 8.14

	✓
True	✓
False	

If an individual has allowable losses brought forward, these are only used to bring gains down to the annual exempt amount.

Task 8.15

The maximum allowable loss carried forward to 2017/18 will be:

£	11,700

Tax year	2014/15 £	2015/16 £	2016/17 £
Gains	2,000	4,000	13,400
Losses	(14,000)	(2,000)	(2,000)
Net gain/(loss)	(12,000)	2,000	11,400
Less loss b/f	(0)	0	(300)
Less annual exempt amount	0	(2,000)	(11,100)
Chargeable gain	0	0	0
Loss c/f	(12,000)	(12,000)	(11,700)

The use of the loss brought forward in 2016/17 is restricted to leave chargeable gains equal to the annual exempt amount.

Task 8.16

	✓
Beatrice	
Susan	
Simon	
Sarah	✓

Mary is connected to her daughter (Beatrice), her sister-in-law (Susan) and her brother-in-law (Simon). Mary is not connected to her niece (Sarah).

Task 8.17

	✓
True	
False	✓

The loss of £(3,000) can only be set against gains on disposals made to the son (ie the same connected person) in the same tax year or future tax years.

Task 8.18

Her chargeable gain on sale is:

£	833

	£
Gross proceeds	6,500
Less costs of sale	(130)
Net proceeds	6,370
Less cost	(1,500)
Chargeable gain	4,870
Gain cannot exceed 5/3 × £(6,500 – 6,000)	833

Task 8.19

Jolyon's allowable loss is:

£	1,125

	£
Deemed proceeds	6,000
Less costs of sale	(125)
Net proceeds	5,875
Less cost	(7,000)
Allowable loss	(1,125)

Task 8.20

	✓
True	
False	✓

Both the proceeds and the cost are less than £6,000 so the gain is exempt.

Task 8.21

Tick to show the chargeable gain on sale of the picture.

	✓
£1,200	
£2,000	
£2,500	✓
£3,700	

	£
Gross proceeds	7,500
Less costs of sale	(300)
Net proceeds	7,200
Less cost	(3,500)
Chargeable gain	3,700
Gain cannot exceed 5/3 × £(7,500 – 6,000)	2,500

Task 8.22

Mark purchased an antique vase for £9,000. He sold the vase in August 2016 at auction for £4,500 net of auctioneer's fees of £500.

Mark's allowable loss is:

£	(3,500)

	£
Deemed proceeds	6,000
Less costs of sale	(500)
Net proceeds	5,500
Less cost	(9,000)
Allowable loss	(3,500)

Chapter 9

Task 9.1

	✓
Against 10,000 of the shares purchased on 10 May 2008	
Against 5,000 of the shares purchased on 24 January 2017 and then against 5,000 of the shares purchased on 10 May 2008	
Against 10,000 of the total shareholding of 20,000 shares	
Against the 8,000 shares purchased on 24 January 2017 and then against 2,000 of the shares purchased on 10 May 2008	✓

Task 9.2

His net chargeable gain on sale is:

£	9,800

Mr Stevens will match his disposal of 5,000 shares on 10 August 2016 to acquisitions as follows:

(1) 1,000 shares bought on 16 August 2016 (next 30 days, FIFO basis)

(2) 4,000 shares from the share pool (which only consists of the 6,000 shares bought in July 2015)

Disposal of 1,000 shares bought on 16 August 2016

	£
Proceeds of sale £20,000 × 1,000/5,000	4,000
Less cost	(4,200)
Allowable loss	(200)

Disposal of 4,000 shares bought from the share pool (= July 2015 acquisition)

	£
Proceeds of sale £20,000 × 4,000/5,000	16,000
Less cost £9,000 × 4,000/6,000	(6,000)
Chargeable gain	10,000
Net chargeable gain = £10,000 – 200	9,800

Task 9.3

Share pool

	No. of shares	Cost £
10 February 2001	12,000	18,000
20 September 2008 Bonus 1:4 (1/4 × 12,000 = 3,000 shares)	3,000	0
	15,000	18,000
15 March 2017 Disposal (£18,000 × 2,000/15,000 = £2,400)	(2,000)	(2,400)
	13,000	15,600

Gain on sale

	£
Proceeds	8,000
Less cost	(2,400)
Gain	5,600

Task 9.4

Mark will match his disposal of 10,000 shares on 4 November 2016 as follows:

(1) 2,000 shares bought on 10 November 2016
(2) 8,000 shares from share pool

Disposal of 2,000 shares bought on 10 November 2016

	£
Proceeds $\frac{2,000}{10,000} \times £60,000$	12,000
Less cost	(11,500)
Chargeable gain	500
Disposal of 8,000 shares from share pool	
Proceeds $\frac{8,000}{10,000} \times £60,000$	48,000
Less cost (W)	(12,200)
Chargeable gain	35,800
Total chargeable gain (£500 + £35,800)	36,300

Share pool working	No. of shares	Cost £
9 December 2001	12,000	4,400
12 October 2005 Rights 1:3 × £5	4,000	20,000
(1/3 × 12,000 = 4,000 shares × £5 = £20,000)		
	16,000	24,400
4 November 2016 Disposal	(8,000)	(12,200)
(£24,400 × 8,000/16,000 = £12,200)		
	8,000	12,200

Task 9.5

	£
Disposal proceeds	3,675,000
Less cost (W)	(537,600)
Chargeable gain	3,137,400

Working: share pool

	Number	Cost £
Purchase June 2006	500,000	960,000
Bonus issue December 2011		
500,000 × 3/2	750,000	0
Disposal September 2016	1,250,000	960,000
960,000 × 700,000/1,250,000	(700,000)	(537,600)
Balance carried forward	550,000	422,400

Chapter 10

Task 10.1

	✓
16.5/25	
8.5/25	
15.5/25	
11.5/25	✓

	Chargeable	Exempt
Actual occupation		8
Employment abroad (actual occupation before and after period of absence) – any period		5
Actual occupation		2
Absence (not followed by period of actual occupation)	8.5	
Last 18 months of ownership		1.5
Totals	8.5	16.5

Task 10.2

	✓
True	✓
False	

The period when the property was unoccupied will be covered by the last 18 months deemed occupation rule.

Task 10.3

	£
Proceeds	180,000
Less cost	(50,000)
Gain before PPR exemption	130,000
Less PPR exemption	(72,222)
Chargeable gain	57,778

Working:

	Exempt years	Chargeable years
1.8.98 – 31.7.01 (actual occupation)	3	
1.8.01 – 31.7.05 (up to 4 years due to place of work not employed abroad)	4	
1.8.05 – 31.7.06 (up to 3 years any reason)	1	
1.8.06 – 31.1.07 (actual occupation)	½	
1.2.07 – 31.1.15 (not followed by actual occupation)		8
1.2.15 – 31.7.16 (last 1½ years)	1½	
Totals	10	8

Task 10.4

	✓
14.5/15	✓
14/15	
13.5/15	
15/15	

	Exempt years	Chargeable years	Total years
Actual occupation	3		3
Deemed occupation – any time employed overseas	5		5
Actual occupation	2		2
Deemed occupation – up to 3 years any reason	3		3
Unoccupied		½	½
Last 18 months of ownership	1½		1½
Totals	14½	½	15

Task 10.5

	✓
True	
False	✓

Periods of time working abroad are only covered by the deemed occupation rules if the owner lives in the property before and after the absence.

AAT AQ2016 SAMPLE ASSESSMENT

Personal Tax

Time allowed: 2.5 hours

AAT AQ2016
SAMPLE ASSESSMENT

Personal Tax (PLTX)
AAT sample assessment 1

Task 1 (10 marks)

You work for a small firm of chartered accountants. One of your colleagues has sent you an email saying that he saw one of your clients working in a carwash and it appeared as though the client owned the carwash. You have checked the client's file and the only business which is being declared to HMRC is a restaurant.

Using the AAT guidelines 'Professional conduct in relation to taxation', explain what steps you should take regarding this possible irregularity.

Task 2 (8 marks)

Sam had the use of two company cars during 2016/17 and his employer paid the running costs for each car, including all fuel. The table below details all of necessary information in respect of each car.

Car	Number of months	List price £	Cost price £	Contribution to the cost made by Sam £	Scale charge %
Car 1	5	28,150	25,130	6,000	27
Car 2	7	18,920	17,100	1,500	19

(a) Complete the following sentences to show Sam's taxable benefit in kind for the cars for 2016/17. Show your answers in whole pounds only.

The benefit in kind for the use of Car 1 for 2016/17 is £ ______.

The benefit in kind for the provision of fuel for Car 1 for 2016/17 is £ ______.

The benefit in kind for the use of Car 2 for 2016/17 is £ ______.

The benefit in kind for the provision of fuel for Car 2 for 2016/17 is £ ______.

(b) Complete the following table by inserting the scale charge for 2016/17 for each of the cars shown below.

	Engine type	CO2 emissions	Scale charge %
Car 3	Petrol	181	
Car 4	Diesel	212	

Task 3 (8 marks)

In the table below is a list of benefits that Clartt Ltd provides to its employees.

Enter the amount that would be taxable for 2016/17 for each benefit in the box provided. If your answer is zero, enter '0'. Enter your answer in whole pounds only.

Details	Taxable benefit in kind £
Joe is a higher rate taxpayer and Clartt Ltd pays £40 per week (for 52 weeks) to a registered childminder for Joe's daughter.	
Jules moved into a house provided by Clartt Ltd on 1 August 2013 when its market value was £320,500. The house cost Clartt Ltd £236,000 in January 2007. The house has an annual value of £6,900. Jules pays Clartt Ltd £750 per month towards the use of the house.	
A television and cinema system costing Clartt Ltd £15,500 was bought for Ranjit's use on 1 September 2016.	
All employees had the use of a subsidised canteen. The cost to Clartt Ltd was £580 per employee.	
George moved 150 miles due to a promotion and received £9,500 to help with his removal expenses.	
On 1 July 2016, James was given a loan of £12,000 on which he paid 3.5% interest. He has not repaid any of this loan yet.	
Margaret had the sole use of a company van throughout all of 2016/17. Clartt Ltd pays for all fuel and 50% of the mileage is for private usage.	

Task 4 (6 marks)

The information below relates to investment income received during 2016/17 by three taxpayers.

Complete the following sentences for each taxpayer. If your answer is zero, enter '0'. Enter your answer in whole pounds only.

Doris received a dividend of £10,000. Her other taxable income, after personal allowances, totalled £21,500.

The tax payable by Doris on these dividends is | £ | |.

Honey received £2,500 in interest from her building society account and £310 in interest from her individual savings account. Her other taxable income, after personal allowances, totalled £45,800.

Honey's income from investments on which tax will be paid is | £ | |.

The total tax payable on this interest by Honey is | £ | |.

Ivanka received building society interest of £3,200. Her other taxable income, after personal allowances, totalled £125,900.

Ivanka's taxable income from investments will be | £ | |.

The total tax payable on this interest by Ivanka is | £ | |.

Task 5 (6 marks)

Sam rented out three properties which he owned for the whole of 2016/17. Information on the properties is shown in the table below.

Complete the table below to show taxable rent and allowable expenses for these properties in 2016/17. If your answer is zero, enter '0'. Enter your answers in whole pounds only.

Property	Details	Taxable rent £	Allowable expenses £
Green Cottage	Green Cottage was let from 1 June 2016 for the remainder of the tax year for £830 per month. Sam paid 10% commission to a letting agent and paid £600 in advertising costs.		
Yellow Gardens	Yellow Gardens was let from 1 January 2017 for the remainder of the tax year at £550 per month. Sam paid £2,850 in August 2016 to replace the single glazed windows with double glazed windows.		
Lime Lane	Lime Lane was let for the whole of 2016/17 at £770 per month. Sam paid for the building insurance, which cost him £600 for the year from 1 January 2016 and £624 for the year from 1 January 2017.		

Task 6 (12 marks)

John has the following income for 2016/17:

	£
Income from employment	58,000
Profits from property	15,500
Building society interest received	1,200
Dividends received	3,000

John has losses from property brought forward of £9,250 from 2015/16.

During 2016/17, John paid £224 per month into a private pension scheme.

(a) Calculate John's total income tax liability for 2016/17, entering your answer and workings in the blank table below.

You have been given more space than you will need.

Joy's only income during 2016/17 was her gross salary of £110,000. She is confused why her personal allowance is only £6,000 for 2016/17.

(b) Clearly explain in the box below why the personal allowance for Joy of £6,000 for 2016/17 is correct.

Task 7 (4 marks)

During 2016/17, Jonny received a gross salary of £58,000 and total benefits in kind (none of which are convertible into cash) of £6,850.

Complete the following sentences by typing your answer, in whole pounds, in the boxes provided. Ignore the employment allowance.

The total Class 1 National Insurance contributions payable by Jonny in 2016/17 are £ ______.

The total Class 1 National Insurance contributions payable by Jonny's employer in 2016/17 are £ ______.

The total Class 1A National Insurance contributions payable by Jonny's employer in 2016/17 are £ ______.

Task 8 (7 marks)

(a) Tick to show if the following statements are true or false.

Statement	True	False
Henry has always wanted to invest in shares but he does not own any. He has just won £4,000 in the lottery, so he decides to invest this win in shares. There will be no income tax implications on this investment.		
An employee is provided with his first £20,000 loan by his employer. For this loan to be tax free, the employer must charge interest above 0%.		

(b) Complete the following sentences.

Michael and Julia are married. For 2016/17, Michael has total employment income of £87,000 and Julia has total employment income of £8,000. Currently, all investments are jointly owned. To minimise their total tax liability, all the investment income should ______ ▼

Drop-down list:

be in Michael's name.
be in Julia's name.
remain in joint names.

Ruby has total income of £105,000. She wants to pay into her private pension scheme so that she can protect her full personal allowances of £11,000. She therefore needs to pay at least | £ | | into her private pension scheme.

Chen is a basic rate taxpayer. He has a company car for the whole of2016/17. It is a Ford car which has a scale charge percentage of 13% and an assessable benefit in kind of £2,431. He has been offered a Volvocar which costs the same as the Ford, but with a scale charge percentage of 7%. If Chen chose the Volvo on 6 April 2016, this will save him | £ | | in income tax for 2016/17.

Task 9 (10 marks)

During 2016/17. Sam sold five assets to unconnected persons. The proceeds and cost of each asset are shown in the table below.

(a) Show whether the selling of each asset below will result in a taxable gain, an allowable loss, or be exempt from capital gains tax, and then indicate the amount of gain/loss in the final column. If you think the asset is exempt, enter a zero '0' in the final column.

Do not leave any cells blank. Do not use brackets or minus signs.

Asset	Proceeds £	Cost £	Taxable gain, allowable loss or exempt?	Amount of gain/loss £
Desk	8,980	7,140	▼	
Chair	6,240	5,600	▼	
Mirror	5,140	6,330	▼	
Ring	3,810	4,600	▼	
Race horse	10,560	5,500	▼	

Drop-down list:

Allowable loss
Exempt
Taxable gain

(b) **Complete the following sentences.**

Robin and his sister-in-law [▼] be treated as connected persons.

Drop-down list:

would
would not

A 70 year old vintage car [▼] be treated as a chargeable asset.

Drop-down list:

would
would not

(c) Elizabeth bought a painting for £32,400 in June 2007 and was charged 10% commission by the auctioneer. She sold the painting in January 2017 for £58,500, spending £1,200 on advertising it for sale.

Throughout the period of ownership, Elizabeth spent £2,200 on insuring the painting.

Complete the following table to show the gain made on the sale of the painting.

Do not use brackets or minus signs.

	£
Proceeds	
Total cost	
Gain	

Task 10 (10 marks)

Keith bought and sold numerous shares in Helle plc as follows:

Event date	Detail
1 January 2011	Keith purchased 800 shares at a cost of £6.10 per share.
1 July 2013	There was a 1 for 5 rights issue at a cost of £3.80 per share.
12 August 2013	Keith sold 400 shares for £8.00 per share.
25 March 2014	There was a 1 for 10 bonus issue when the shares had a market value of £6.90 each.
14 April 2014	Keith bought 500 shares at a cost of £8.20 per share.
19 October 2016	Keith sold 250 shares for £10.10 per share.

Clearly showing the balance of shares and their value to carry forward, calculate the gain Keith made on the sale of the shares for 2016/17.

All workings must be shown in your calculations.

Task 11 (7 marks)

The following information is available about four taxpayers who sold capital assets during 2016/17.

These are the only assets that they sold during 2016/17, none of which relate to residential property.

Taxpayer	Sold to	Proceeds £	Market value £	Cost £	Other taxable income £
Alex	Husband	28,750	42,600	12,000	47,500
Donna	Brother	19,000	22,000	7,500	30,000
Carl	Stranger	64,800	64,000	44,050	54,600
Bridget	Friend	26,000	28,000	9,500	18,430

Calculate the amount of capital gains tax payable for each taxpayer. Your answer must be in whole pounds only. If your answer is zero, enter '0'.

The amount of capital gains tax payable by Alex is £ ______.

The amount of capital gains tax payable by Donna is £ ______.

The amount of capital gains tax payable by Carl is £ ______.

The amount of capital gains tax payable by Bridget is £ ______.

Task 12 (6 marks)

(a) Complete the following sentences that relate to inheritance tax (IHT). If appropriate, enter your answer in whole pounds only. If your answer is zero, enter '0'.

Richard transferred the ownership of a boat into his wife's name in May 2013. In December 2016, Richard died. The transfer of the boat ______ ▼ be exempt from IHT on Richard's death.

Drop-down list:

would
would not

Samantha received £10,000 from her grandfather on the occasion of her marriage on 22 March 2017. The maximum value of the transfer that may be liable to IHT when her grandfather dies is | £ | |.

An individual who is domiciled in the UK could be liable to IHT on their estate which is situated [▼].

Drop-down list:

in the UK only
anywhere in the world

An individual who is not domiciled in the UK could be liable to IHT on their estate which is situated [▼].

Drop-down list:

in the UK only
anywhere in the world

(b) Tick to show if the following statements are true or false.

Statement	True	False
Partnerships are treated as chargeable persons for IHT purposes.		
The £250 small gift exemption is per transferee per tax year.		

Task 13 (6 marks)

Ian died on 12 January 2017 leaving an estate valued at £2,200,000.

His will shows that the entire estate is to be left to his grandchildren and he made no gifts during his lifetime.

Ian's wife died on 22 September 2010. Her estate on death used 30% of the nil rate tax band.

(a) Calculate the inheritance tax payable on Ian's estate, entering your answer and workings into the blank table below. You have been given more space than you will need.

AAT AQ2016 SAMPLE ASSESSMENT
Personal Tax

ANSWERS

BPP LEARNING MEDIA

Personal Tax (PLTX)
AAT sample assessment 1

Task 1 (10 marks)

Using the AAT guidelines 'Professional conduct in relation to taxation', explain what steps you should take regarding this possible irregularity.

Firstly, the facts need to be established. Was the client working in the carwash? Is he the owner? If not (maybe helping a friend out when on holiday and not being paid) then no further action needs to be taken. However, if there does appear to be an irregularity, is the amount involved trivial? It would suggest not, in which case the client needs to be approached to find out the facts.

If indeed the client has monetary gains from the carwash, then they must be advised that it needs to be disclosed to HMRC. If the client agrees to disclose to HMRC this business, then the client needs to be advised on the potential for penalties, interest, surcharges and other consequences. If the client does not agree to disclose, then the client needs to be advised on the consequences of failure to disclose. Such advice needs to be done in writing.

If the client still does not agree to disclose to HMRC, then you must cease to act for the client and inform HMRC of the withdrawal. However, because of the need to maintain client confidentiality, HMRC should not be provided with an explanation of the reasons why you have ceased to act.

Task 2 (8 marks)

(a) Complete the following sentences to show Sam's taxable benefit in kind for the cars for 2016/17. Show your answers in whole pounds only.

The benefit in kind for the use of Car 1 for 2016/17 is £ 2,604.

The benefit in kind for the provision of fuel for Car 1 for 2016/17 is £ 2,497.

The benefit in kind for the use of Car 2 for 2016/17 is £ 1,930.

The benefit in kind for the provision of fuel for Car 2 for 2016/17 is £ 2,460.

(b) Complete the following table by inserting the scale charge for 2016/17 for each of the cars shown below.

	Engine type	CO2 emissions	Scale charge %
Car 3	Petrol	181	33
Car 4	Diesel	212	37

Task 3 (8 marks)

Enter the amount that would be taxable for 2016/17 for each benefit in the box provided. If your answer is zero, enter '0'. Enter your answer in whole pounds only.

Details	Taxable benefit in kind £
Joe is a higher rate taxpayer and Clartt Ltd pays £40 per week (for 52 weeks) to a registered childminder for Joe's daughter.	624
Jules moved into a house provided by Clartt Ltd on 1 August 2013 when its market value was £320,500. The house cost Clartt Ltd £236,000 in January 2007. The house has an annual value of £6,900. Jules pays Clartt Ltd £750 per month towards the use of the house.	5,265
A television and cinema system costing Clartt Ltd £15,500 was bought for Ranjit's use on 1 September 2016.	1,808
All employees had the use of a subsidised canteen. The cost to Clartt Ltd was £580 per employee.	0
George moved 150 miles due to a promotion and received £9,500 to help with his removal expenses.	1,500
On 1 July 2016, James was given a loan of £12,000 on which he paid 3.5% interest. He has not repaid any of this loan yet.	0
Margaret had the sole use of a company van throughout all of 2016/17. Clartt Ltd pays for all fuel and 50% of the mileage is for private usage.	3,768

Task 4 (6 marks)

Complete the following sentences for each taxpayer. If your answer is zero, enter '0'. Enter your answer in whole pounds only.

Doris received a dividend of £10,000. Her other taxable income, after personal allowances, totalled £21,500.

The tax payable by Doris on these dividends is | £ | 375 |.

Honey received £2,500 in interest from her building society account and £310 in interest from her individual savings account. Her other taxable income, after personal allowances, totalled £45,800.

Honey's income from investments on which tax will be paid is | £ | 2,000 |.

The total tax payable on this interest by Honey is | £ | 800 |.

Ivanka received building society interest of £3,200. Her other taxable income, after personal allowances, totalled £125,900.

Ivanka's taxable income from investments will be | £ | 2,700 |.

The total tax payable on this interest by Ivanka is | £ | 1,080 |.

Task 5 (6 marks)

Complete the table below to show taxable rent and allowable expenses for these properties in 2016/17. If your answer is zero, enter '0'. Enter your answers in whole pounds only.

Property	Details	Taxable rent £	Allowable expenses £
Green Cottage	Green Cottage was let from 1 June 2016 for the remainder of the tax year for £830 per month. Sam paid 10% commission to a letting agent and paid £600 in advertising costs.	8,300	1,430
Yellow Gardens	Yellow Gardens was let from 1 January 2017 for the remainder of the tax year at £550 per month. Sam paid £2,850 in August 2016 to replace the single glazed windows with double glazed windows.	1,650	2,850
Lime Lane	Lime Lane was let for the whole of 2016/17 at £770 per month. Sam paid for the building insurance, which cost him £600 for the year from 1 January 2016 and £624 for the year from 1 January 2017.	9,240	606

Task 6 (12 marks)

(a) Calculate John's total income tax liability for 2016/17, entering your answer and workings in the blank table below.

You have been given more space than you will need.

		£
Employment income		58,000
Property income	(£15,500 – £9,250)	6,250
Building society interest		1,200
Dividends		3,000
		68,450
Personal allowance		11,000
		57,450
Basic rate: £32,000 + (£224 × 12 × 100/80) = £35,360		
£35,360 × 20%		7,072
£17,890 × 40%	(£57,450 – £35,360 – £4,200)	7,156
£700 × 40%	(£1,200 – £500)	280
Dividends	Below £5,000	0
Total		14,508

(b) Clearly explain in the box below why the personal allowance for Joy of £6,000 for 2016/17 is correct.

As Joy has total income over £100,000 her personal allowance will be reduced by £1 for every £2 over £100,000.

Therefore, the computation for her personal allowance would be £11,000 – ((£110,000 – £100,000)/2) = £6,000.

Task 7 (4 marks)

Complete the following sentences by typing your answer, in whole pounds, in the boxes provided. Ignore the employment allowance.

The total Class 1 National Insurance contributions payable by Jonny in 2016/17 are | £ | 4,492 |.

The total Class 1 National Insurance contributions payable by Jonny's employerin 2016/17 are | £ | 6,884 |.

The total Class 1A National Insurance contributions payable by Jonny's employerin 2016/17 are | £ | 945 |.

Task 8 (7 marks)

(a) Tick to show if the following statements are true or false.

Statement	True	False
Henry has always wanted to invest in shares but he does not own any. He has just won £4,000 in the lottery, so he decides to invest this win in shares. There will be no income tax implications on this investment.	✓	
An employee is provided with his first £20,000 loan by his employer. For this loan to be tax free, the employer must charge interest above 0%.		✓

(b) Complete the following sentences.

Michael and Julia are married. For 2016/17, Michael has total employment income of £87,000 and Julia has total employment income of £8,000. Currently, all investments are jointly owned. To minimise their total tax liability, all the investment income should | be in Julia's name. |

Ruby has total income of £105,000. She wants to pay into her private pension scheme so that she can protect her full personal allowances of £11,000. She therefore needs to pay at least | £ | 4,000 | into her private pension scheme.

Chen is a basic rate taxpayer. He has a company car for the whole of 2016/17. It is a Ford car which has a scale charge percentage of 13% and an assessable benefit in kind of £2,431. He has been offered a Volvocar which costs the same as the Ford, but with a scale charge percentage of 7%. If Chen chose the Volvo on 6 April 2016, this will save him | £ | 224 | in income tax for 2016/17.

Note. This model answer shows the figure rounded down, however figures rounded up are equally valid for the purposes of this assessment.

Task 9 (10 marks)

(a) Show whether the selling of each asset below will result in a taxable gain, an allowable loss or be exempt from capital gains tax, and then indicate the amount of gain/loss in the final column. If you think the asset is exempt, enter a zero '0' in the final column.

Do not leave any cells blank. Do not use brackets or minus signs.

Asset	Proceeds £	Cost £	Taxable gain, allowable loss or exempt?	Amount of gain/loss £
Desk	8,980	7,140	Taxable gain	1,840
Chair	6,240	5,600	Taxable gain	400
Mirror	5,140	6,330	Allowable loss	330
Ring	3,810	4,600	Exempt	0
Race horse	10,560	5,500	Exempt	0

(b) Complete the following sentences.

Robin and his sister-in-law | would | be treated as connected persons.

A 70 year old vintage car | would not | be treated as a chargeable asset.

(c) Complete the following table to show the gain made on the sale of the painting.Do not use brackets or minus signs.

	£
Proceeds	58,500
Total cost	36,840
Gain	21,660

Task 10 (10 marks)

Clearly showing the balance of shares and their value to carry forward, calculate the gain Keith made on the sale of the shares for 2016/17.

All workings must be shown in your calculations.

	Event	Shares	£
1 January 2011	Purchase	800	4,880
1 July 2013	Right issue	160	608
		960	5,488
12 August 2013	Disposal	(400)	2,287
		560	3,201
25 March 2014	Bonus issue	56	0
		616	3,201
14 April 2014	Purchase	500	4,100
		1,116	7,301
19 October 2016	Disposal	(250)	1,636
Pool to carry forward		866	5,665
Proceeds		2,525	
Cost		1,636	
Gain		889	

Task 11 (7 marks)

Calculate the amount of capital gains tax payable for each taxpayer. Your answer must be in whole pounds only. If your answer is zero, enter '0'.

The amount of capital gains tax payable by Alex is | £ | 0 |.

The amount of capital gains tax payable by Donna is | £ | 480 |.

The amount of capital gains tax payable by Carl is | £ | 1,930 |.

The amount of capital gains tax payable by Bridget is | £ | 540 |.

Task 12 (6 marks)

(a) Complete the following sentences that relate to inheritance tax (IHT). If appropriate, enter your answer in whole pounds only. If your answer is zero, enter '0'.

Richard transferred the ownership of a boat into his wife's name in May 2013. In December 2016, Richard died. The transfer of the boat [would] be exempt from IHT on Richard's death.

Samantha received £10,000 from her grandfather on the occasion of her marriage on 22 March 2017. The maximum value of the transfer that may be liable to IHT when her grandfather dies is | £ | 7,500 |.

An individual who is domiciled in the UK could be liable to IHT on their estate which is situated [anywhere in the world].

An individual who is not domiciled in the UK could be liable to IHT on their estate which is situated [in the UK only].

(b) Tick show if the following statements are true or false.

Statement	True	False
Partnerships are treated as chargeable persons for IHT purposes.		✓
The £250 small gift exemption is per transferee per tax year.	✓	

Task 13 (6 marks)

(a) Calculate the inheritance tax payable on Ian's estate, entering your answer and workings into the blank table below. You have been given more space than you will need.

	Workings:	£
Chargeable estate		2,200,000
Nil rate band:	Ian	325,000
	Ian's wife (£325,000 × 70%)	227,500
		552,500
Taxable:	£2,200,000 – £552,500	1,647,500
Tax payable:	@40%	659,000

AAT AQ2016 SAMPLE ASSESSMENT 2
Personal Tax

You are advised to attempt sample assessment 2 online from the AAT website. This will ensure you are prepared for how the assessment will be presented on the AAT's system when you attempt the real assessment. Please access the assessment using the address below:

https://www.aat.org.uk/training/study-support/search

BPP PRACTICE ASSESSMENT 1 PERSONAL TAX

Time allowed: 2.5 hours

PRACTICE ASSESSMENT 1

Personal Tax (PLTX)
BPP practice assessment 1

Task 1

You work for a firm of accountants. A few weeks ago, you prepared a tax return for Sharon. Sharon has now told you that she forgot to include some bank interest in the return but that she does not intend to tell HM Revenue & Customs (HMRC) of the omission.

Explain what steps you should take regarding this information.

Task 2

Shane is provided with a company car for business and private use throughout 2016/17. The car had a list price of £16,700 when bought new in December 2013, although the company paid £15,000 for the car after a dealer discount. It has a petrol engine, with CO_2 emissions of 134g/km. The company pays for all running costs, including all fuel. Shane does not make any contribution for his private use of the car.

(a) The cost of the car in the taxable benefit computation is:

£	

(b) The percentage used in the taxable benefit computation is:

	%

(c) The taxable benefit in respect of the provision of fuel for private use is:

£	

Task 3

(a) Josie is a basic rate taxpayer and receives the following benefits as the result of her employment.

In each case enter the taxable benefit arising in 2016/17. If the benefit is exempt, enter 0.

(1) A mobile telephone for private and business use throughout the year. The purchase of the phone and the calls from it cost her employer a total of £350 for 2016/17.

£	

(2) Childcare vouchers of £100 per week for 48 weeks during 2016/17.

£	

(3) Leisure club membership for Josie costing her employer £5,000 using a corporate discount scheme. If a member of the public had taken this membership it would have cost £6,500.

£	

(4) Use of a house near her work that enables her to start work at 7.00am every morning. The house has an annual value of £5,900 and cost her employer £227,000 4 years ago.

£	

(b) For each of the following benefits, tick whether they would be wholly or partly taxable or wholly exempt if received in 2016/17:

Item	Wholly or partly taxable	Wholly exempt
Interest on loan of £8,000 (only loan provided)		
Additional costs of home working of £5 per week (no evidence presented to employer)		
Use of pool car		
One staff party costing £120 per head		

Task 4

During 2016/17, Eva received the following income.

In each case, show the amount of income that she should enter on her tax return. If the income is exempt, enter 0.

(a) Employment income £20,000, tax deducted £2,700.

£	

(b) Government stock ('gilt') interest £40.

£	

(c) Interest on ISA account £90.

£	

(d) Dividends received £1,280.

£	

Task 5

(a) Emily lets a furnished house for £150 a week. During 2016/17 the flat was let for 40 weeks. It was unoccupied for the remaining 12 weeks of the year.

During 2016/17, Emily spent £190 on advertising for tenants, £460 on water rates, £800 on redecoration, £690 on electricity and £368 on cleaning. Emily also installed a new central heating system at a cost of £1,200. Previously, the house did not have central heating. Emily replaced some furniture at a cost of £554 during 2016/17.

Calculate the property income taxable on Emily for 2016/17 using the proforma layout provided. Fill in all the unshaded boxes. If any item is not an allowable expense, enter 0. Both brackets and minus signs can be used to show negative numbers.

	£
Rent	
Expenses:	
Advertising	
Water rates	
Redecoration	
Electricity	
Cleaning	
Central heating system	
Furniture cost	
Property income	

(b) Oliver and George jointly own a house, which is their main residence. They let out one of the rooms to Julie.

What is the maximum exempt amount to which Oliver and George are each entitled under rent a room relief?

	✓
£3,000	
£3,750	
£6,000	
£7,500	

Task 6

Denise works for Jules Ltd. She provides you with the following information:

(1) Annual salary £104,000 received on 25th day of each month.

(2) Employer's contribution of 5% of salary on 31 December 2016 to company's occupational pension scheme. Denise contributes 4% of her salary into this scheme.

(3) Bonus of £1,000 received 30 April 2016 based on company's accounting profit for the year ended 31 December 2015.

(4) Bonus of £1,200 received 30 April 2017 based on company's accounting profit for the year ended 31 December 2016.

(5) She has use of a company car for which the benefit in kind has been computed as £3,000. Denise pays for all the private petrol that she uses in this car.

(6) During 2016/17 Denise received £150 of bank interest and £50 of dividends from an ISA.

Complete the following table showing the figures that should be included in Denise's taxable income for 2016/17. You should use whole pounds only. If your answer is zero, please input a '0'. Do not use brackets or minus signs.

	£
Salary	
Employer's pension contribution	
Employee's pension contribution	
Bonus received 30 April 2016	
Bonus received 30 April 2017	
Benefit in kind for car	
Interest from bank	
Dividends from ISA	
Total income	
Personal allowance	
Taxable income	

Task 7

(a) Elaine was born in 1968. During 2016/17 she earned £115,000 of employment income and received bank interest of £5,000 and dividends of £18,000.

Calculate her total income tax liability to the nearest pound for 2016/17, entering your answer and workings in the blank table given below. You have been given more space than you will need.

(b) Elaine is considering making a Gift Aid donation of £500 each year to a charity. However she does not understand the tax implications of doing this.

Explain to Elaine how she will get tax relief on such donations, and the tax implications if she had made a £500 Gift Aid donation during 2016/17.

Task 8

A recently retired client has approached your manager about the tax planning opportunities available for inheritance tax.

Please could you write some notes for your manager's meeting with the client.

Task 9

(a) For each of the following assets, tick whether they are chargeable or exempt assets for capital gains tax:

Asset	Chargeable	Exempt
Car used solely for business purposes		
Holiday cottage		
Vintage car worth £40,000		
Shares held in an individual savings account		

(b) Rodney purchased an antique chair for £1,450. On 10 October 2016 he sold the chair at auction for £6,300 (which was net of the auctioneer's 10% commission).

The chargeable gain on sale is:

£	

(c) Andrew bought six acres of land for £405,000. He sold two acres of the land at auction for £360,000. His disposal costs were £6,000. The market value of the four remaining acres at the date of sale was £540,000.

(1) The cost of the land sold is:

£	

(2) The chargeable gain on sale is:

£	

Task 10

In August 2010 Wayne acquired 4,000 shares in Main plc at a cost of £10,000. In September 2012, there was a one for one bonus issue when the shares were worth £8 each. Wayne sold 3,000 shares in July 2013 for £15,000, and purchased 3,000 back againin October 2013 for £12,000.

Wayne sold half of his shareholding in June 2016 for £21,000.

Clearly showing the balance of shares and their value to carry forward, calculate the gain made on the sale of the shares in 2016/17. All workings must be shown in your calculations.

Task 11

(a) For each of the following statements, tick if they are True or False.

	True	False
Any CGT annual exempt amount that is unused in one tax year can be carried forward to be used in the following tax year only.		
Capital losses in a tax year must be offset against capital gains in that year, even if it means losing all, or some of the annual exempt amount.		

(b) Charlotte bought a house on 1 February 2004 for £95,000 and sold it for £263,000 on 1 October 2016. During the period of ownership the following occurred:

01.02.04 to 31.10.06	Charlotte lived in the property
01.11.06 to 31.03.15	Charlotte worked elsewhere in the UK
01.04.15 to 30.09.16	Charlotte lived in the property until she sold it

Input the correct answers in the boxes provided to complete the sentences. Where applicable round your answer to the nearest whole number.

The total period of ownership of the property is [ ] months.

The period of Charlotte's actual and deemed residence is [ ] months.

The chargeable gain on the sale of the house is [ ].

(c) Ella purchased an antique clock for £12,000. She sold it on 1 September 2016 for £62,100. Ella has no other chargeable assets. Her taxable income for 2016/17 was £29,000.

Ella's CGT payable for 2016/17 is:

£	

This is payable by (xx/xx/xxxx):

Task 12

(a) Andy and Hilda had been married for many years when Andy died in June 2009. 60% of Andy's nil rate band was unused on his death. The nil rate band at Andy's death was £325,000. Hilda died in December 2016. Her only lifetime transfers of value were cash gifts of £6,000 to her nephew in January 2016 and £10,000 to her niece in March 2016.

What is the maximum nil rate band available for use against Hilda's death estate?

£	

(b) **For each of the following statements, tick if they are true or false.**

	True	False
A CLT is only chargeable on death of the donor.		
Cars are exempt from IHT.		
The annual exemption for the current year is used before any unused annual exemption brought forward from the prior year.		

Task 13

Jessica made a gross chargeable lifetime transfer of £60,000 (after exemptions) in August 2014. In November 2016, she gave £400,000 to a trust for the benefit of her son. Jessica agreed to pay any lifetime IHT due.

How much inheritance tax will be payable by Jessica on the transfer of value in November 2016?

BPP PRACTICE ASSESSMENT 1 PERSONAL TAX

ANSWERS

Personal Tax (PLTX) BPP practice assessment 1

Task 1

You should inform Sharon of the implications of not reporting this income to HMRC and that it could be viewed as tax evasion which is punishable by fines/imprisonment.

If she refuses to inform HMRC of this income then you should let her know, in writing, that it is not possible for your firm to continue to act for her.

You should then inform HMRC that your firm is no longer acting for Sharon but you should not give details of why you are ceasing to act as this would be a breach of confidentiality.

You should then make a report to your firm's Money Laundering Reporting Officer of Sharon's refusal to disclose the omission to HMRC and the facts surrounding it.

Task 2

(a) The cost of the car in the taxable benefit computation is:

£	16,700

(b) The percentage used in the taxable benefit computation is:

23	**%**

(130 – 95)/5 = 7% + 16% = 23%

(c) The taxable benefit in respect of the provision of fuel for private use is:

£	5,106

£22,200 × 23%

Task 3

(a) **(1)** Mobile telephone

£	0

(2) Childcare vouchers

£	2,160

£(100 – 55) × 48

(3) Leisure club membership (cost to employer)

£	5,000

(4) Home (£5,900 + ((£227,000 – 75,000) × 3%))

£	10,460

(b)

Item	Wholly or partly taxable	Wholly exempt
Interest on loan of £8,000 (only loan provided)		✓(£10,000 or less)
Additional costs of home working of £5 per week (no evidence presented to employer)	✓(evidence needed if more than £4 per week)	
Use of pool car		✓
One staff party costing £120 per head		✓(up to £150)

Task 4

(a) Employment income £20,000, tax deducted £2,700.

£	20,000

(b) Government stock ('gilt') interest £40.

£	40

(c) Interest on ISA account £90.

£	0

Exempt

(d) Dividends received £1,280.

£	1,280

Task 5

(a)

	£
Rentaccrued £150 × 40	6,000
Expenses:	
Advertising	(190)
Water rates	(460)
Redecoration	(800)
Electricity	(690)
Cleaning	(368)
Central heating system (capital)	(0)
Furniture cost	(554)
Property income	2,938

(b)

	✓
£3,000	
£3,750	✓
£6,000	
£7,500	

The rent a room limit of £7,500 is halved if any other person also receives income from renting accommodation in the property.

Task 6

	£
Salary	104,000
Employer's pension contribution (exempt)	0
Employee's pension contribution (£104,000 × 4%)	4,160
Bonus received 30 April 2016	1,000
Bonus received 30 April 2017	0
Benefit in kind for car	3,000
Interest from bank	150
Dividends from ISA (exempt)	0
Total income	103,990
Personal allowance £(11,000 – 1,995 ((103,990 – 100,000)/2))	9,005
Taxable income	94,985

Task 7

(a)

	Non-savings £	Interest £	Dividends £
Employment Income	115,000		
Bank interest		5,000	
Dividends			18,000
Net income	115,000	5,000	18,000
Personal allowance (net income > £122,000)	(nil)		
Taxable income	115,000	5,000	18,000

	Non-savings £	Interest £	Dividends £
£32,000 × 20%	6,400		
£83,000 (£115,000 – £32,000) × 40%	33,200		
£500 × 0% + £4,500 × 40%	1,800		
£5,000 × 0% + £13,000 × 32.5%	4,225		
Income tax liability	45,625		

(b)

If you make a Gift Aid donation of £500 each year to charity this amount will be grossed up at the basic rate of tax, giving a gross amount of £625.

This gross figure of £625 will be used to extend the upper limit of the basic rate band to give an upper limit of £32,625 (£32,000 + £625) and will also extend the additional rate threshold to £150,625 (£150,000 + £625).

This would mean that an extra £625 of your employment income would be taxed at the basic rate of tax of 20% instead of at the higher rate of tax of 40%.

Task 8

Inheritance tax planning:

Gift assets during lifetime to make use of available exemptions such as the marriage and annual exemptions.

Gift assets early – gifts, except gifts to trusts, are exempt from IHT if the donor survives for more than seven years from the date of the gift. Should the donor die within seven years but at least three years after the gift then taper relief applies to reduce the amount of tax payable.

Avoid making gifts to trusts in excess of the available nil band, as these generate an immediate charge to IHT.

Use the nil rate band effectively every seven years.

Ensure the annual exemption is fully utilised.

Make use of the spouse/civil partner exemption and transfer assets to the younger spouse so that they can gift them and hopefully they will then be exempt by the seven year rule.

Task 9

(a)

Asset	Chargeable	Exempt
Car used solely for business purposes		✓
Holiday cottage	✓	
Vintage car worth £40,000		✓
Shares held in an individual savings account		✓

(b) The chargeable gain on sale is:

£	1,667

	£
Disposal proceeds £6,300 × 100/90	7,000
Less disposal costs £7,000 × 10%	(700)
Net proceeds	6,300
Less cost	(1,450)
Gain	4,850
Cannot exceed 5/3 × £(7,000 – 6,000)	1,667

(c) **(1)** The cost of the land sold is:

£	162,000

$$\frac{360{,}000}{360{,}000 + 540{,}000} \times £405{,}000$$

(2) The chargeable gain on sale is:

£	192,000

	£
Disposal proceeds	360,000
Less disposal costs	(6,000)
Net proceeds	354,000
Less cost	(162,000)
Chargeable gain	192,000

Task 10

	£
Proceeds of sale	21,000
Less cost	(9,125)
Gain	11,875

	No. of shares	Cost £
August 2010 Acquisition	4,000	10,000
September 2012 Bonus 1 for 1	4,000	nil
	8,000	10,000
July 2013 Disposal (3,000/8,000 × £10,000)	(3,000)	(3,750)
	5,000	6,250
October 2013 Acquisition	3,000	12,000
	8,000	18,250
June 2016 Disposal (4,000/8,000 × £18,250)	(4,000)	(9,125)
c/f	4,000	9,125

Task 11

(a)

	True	False
Any CGT annual exempt amount that is unused in one tax year can be carried forward to be used in the following tax year only.		✓
Capital losses in a tax year must be offset against capital gains in that year, even if it means losing all, or some of the annual exempt amount.	✓	

Any unused annual exempt amount is lost.

Only capital losses brought forward can be restricted to ensure the annual exempt amount isn't lost.

(b) The total period of ownership of the property is [152] months.

The period of Charlotte's actual and deemed residence is [135] months.

01.02.04 – 31.10.06	33 months actual occupation
01.11.06 – 31.03.15	48 months – deemed occupation – working elsewhere in UK – preceded and followed by actual occupation
	36 months – deemed occupation – any reason – preceded and followed by actual occupation
	17 months non-occupation
01.04.15 – 30.09.16	18 months – actual occupation (last 18 months always deemed occupation anyway)

The chargeable gain on the sale of the house is [£18,789].

	£
Disposal proceeds	263,000
Less cost	(95,000)
	168,000
PPR £168,000 × 135/152	(149,211)
Chargeable gain	18,789

(c) Ella's CGT payable for 2016/17 is:

£	7,500

This is payable by:

31/01/2018

	£
Disposal proceeds	62,100
Less cost	(12,000)
Gain	50,100
Less annual exempt amount	(11,100)
Taxable gain	39,000
CGT	
On £3,000 × 10% (unused basic rate band £32,000 – £29,000)	300
On £36,000 × 20%	7,200
	7,500

Task 12

(a)

£	510,000

	£
Andy's unused nil band: (60% × £325,000)	195,000
Hilda's nil band at death (325,000 – 10,000)	315,000
Total nil band available to Hilda	510,000

(b)

	True	False
A CLT is only chargeable on death of the donor.		✓
Cars are exempt from IHT.		✓
The annual exemption for the current year is used before any unused annual exemption brought forward from the prior year.	✓	

Task 13

	£
Gift	400,000
Less AEs 2016/17, 2015/16 b/f	(6,000)
Net chargeable transfer	394,000
Less nil band remaining £(325,000 – 60,000)	(265,000)
	129,000
IHT @ 20/80	32,250

BPP PRACTICE ASSESSMENT 2
PERSONAL TAX

Time allowed: 2.5 hours

PRACTICE ASSESSMENT 2

Personal Tax (PLTX)
BPP practice assessment 2

Task 1

(a) Steel Ltd provides Susan with two company cars during 2016/17 for private and business use. The first car cost £13,800 when new, has CO_2 emissions of 110g/km and has a diesel engine. The second car has a list price of £12,000, has CO_2 emissions of 90g/km and has a petrol engine. Susan used the first car for the first 7 months of 2016/17, and the second car for the remaining 5 months. Steel Ltd pays for all the running costs which amount to £950 for the first car and £735 for the second car. Steel also paid for private fuel for the second car, however Susan had to contribute £20 per month towards this.

(1) The scale charge percentage for the first car is:

	%

(2) The taxable benefit for the first car is:

£	

(3) The scale charge percentage for the second car is:

	%

(4) The taxable benefit for the second car is:

£	

(5) The fuel benefit for the second car is:

£	

(b) Which fundamental principle does the following describe?
(Please use the picklist below part (c) to answer this question)

To maintain professional knowledge and skill at the level required to ensure that a client or employer receives competent professional service based on current developments in practice, legislation and techniques and acts diligently and in accordance with applicable technical and professional standards.

▼

(c) Discussing client affairs with your friend in the pub who is thinking of investing in the client's company would be a breach of which fundamental principle?

[▼]

Picklist for questions (b) and (c)

Confidentiality
Integrity
Objectivity
Professional behaviour
Professional competence and due care

Task 2

(a) Which ONE of the following is not a wholly exempt employment benefit?

	✓
Long service award of £900 to employee with 30 years of service	
Workplace parking	
Workplace childcare facilities	
Moving expenses of £10,000	

(b) For each of the following benefits provided to Emily by her employer Bloom Ltd, calculate the amount of the taxable benefit for 2016/17. If a benefit is exempt, enter 0.

(1) Bloom Ltd gave Emily a loan on 1 August 2016 of £6,000 to pay for home improvements. Emily pays the company 1% interest on the loan, but has not repaid any of the loan itself.

The taxable benefit for 2016/17 is:

£	

(2) On 1 May 2016 Bloom Ltd provided her with a mobile telephone costing £150 for private and business use.

The taxable benefit for 2016/17 is:

£	

(c) Bella's employer provided her with a house on 1 April 2016, when it was valued at £125,000. The employer had bought the house for £80,000 on 1 April 2007. The annual value of the house is £1,500. Bella pays £75 a month to the employer for the use of the house. She is also provided with new furniture valued at £15,000 on 1 April 2016.

(1) The basic accommodation benefit for 2016/17 is:

£	

(2) The cost of providing the accommodation for calculating the additional benefit is:

£	

(3) The additional accommodation benefit for 2016/17 is:

£	

(4) The benefit for provision of furniture for 2016/17 is:

£	

Task 3

Gavin is employed by XYZ plc.

For each of the following payments, state the amount of employment income taxable in 2016/17. If an amount is not taxable in 2016/17 enter 0.

(a) Annual salary received in monthly payments on the last working day of each month. Until the end of December 2016, his annual salary was £36,000. He had a 2% annual pay increase with effect from 1 January 2017.

The salary to be included in employment income for 2016/17 is:

£	

(b) Bonus of £2,000 received 31 March 2017 based on company's accounting profit for the year ended 31 December 2016.

The bonus to be included in employment income for 2016/17 is:

£	

(c) Commission of £500 received 30 April 2017 on sales made in the month of March 2017.

The commission to be included in employment income for 2016/17 is:

£	

(d) Employer's contribution of £5,000 on 10 March 2017 towards Gavin's occupational pension scheme.

The benefit to be included in employment income for 2016/17 is:

£	

Task 4

(a) Sarah is a higher rate taxpayer and receives total dividends of £7,500 during 2016/17.

(1) The amount of the dividend not taxed at 0% is:

£	

(2) The tax rate applicable to the amount in (1) is:

	%

(3) The income tax payable on the dividend income is (to the nearest £1):

£	

(b) Paul is a basic rate taxpayer and receives interest of £5,000 from an ISA and £3,500 of building society interest during 2016/17.

(1) His personal savings allowance is:

£	

(2) His taxable savings income after the savings allowance is:

£	

(3) The income tax payable on his savings income for 2016/17 is:

£	

Task 5

(a) Demi bought two properties on 1 July 2016.

Property 1 was let unfurnished from 1 September 2016 at an annual rent of £12,000 payable monthly in arrears. The rent due on 31 March 2017 was not received until 14 April 2017.

The following were expenses paid by Demi on the property:

		£
1 July 2016	Insurance for the year ended 30 June 2017	700
8 Sept 2016	Accountancy fees	100
25 January 2017	Re-painting the exterior of the property	400

Property 2 was let furnished from 1 August 2016 at an annual rent of £9,000 payable annually in advance.

The following were expenses paid by Demi on the property:

		£
1 July 2016	Insurance for the year ended 30 June 2017	800
31 March 2017	Redecoration	900
3 April 2017	Purchase of replacement carpets and curtains	600

Using the proforma layout provided, calculate Demi's property income for the tax year 2016/17 by filling in the unshaded boxes. Add zeros if necessary. Both brackets and minus signs can be used to show negative numbers.

	Property 1 £	Property 2 £
Rental income		
Property 1		
Property 2		
Less expenses		
Insurance		
Accountancy		
Repainting		
Redecoration		
Replacement carpets and curtains		
Net income		
Total property income 2016/17		

(b) On which expenditure could Demi claim replacement furniture relief? (Tick all that apply)

	✓
A new fridge to replace the one that stopped working last week	
A television for the new conservatory	
New carpet for the living room after the old one was damaged in the recent floods	
New crockery for the kitchen to replace the chipped plates and bowls	

Task 6

(a) Donald has the following amounts of taxable income for 2016/17:

Non-savings income £152,395 (PAYE deducted £52,000)
Savings income £145
Dividend income £210

Donald's tax liability on each source of income for 2016/17 is as follows:

(1) Non-savings income:

£	

(2) Savings income:

£	

(3) Dividend income:

£	

(4) Donald's tax payable for 2016/17 is:

£	

(b) You have received the following email from Serena Miles:

From:	SMiles@webmail.net
To:	AATStudent@boxmail.net
Sent:	30 November 2017
Subject:	Pensions

I currently don't have a pension and I am worried about this. I have two options. My employer, ABC plc, has said that I can join their occupational pension scheme. This would involve me paying 5% of my basic salary, and they would pay another 7%. However, I don't know how long I am going to continue to work for them.

Alternatively, I am thinking of taking out a private pension, possibly paying about 6% of my earnings into it.

However, I have no idea about the tax implications of these schemes. Would I get tax relief, and if so, how?

I hope you can help.

Serena

WITHOUT discussing the merits of each scheme, advise Serena on the tax implications of an occupational pension scheme and a private pension scheme.

From:	AATStudent@boxmail.net
To:	SMiles@webmail.net
Sent:	1 December 2017
Subject:	Pensions

Task 7

(a) Your client Jackie, who was born in March 1969, received the following income in 2016/17:

	£
Trading income	20,000
Property income	5,000
Building society interest	145
Interest from government stocks	180
Dividends from an ISA	204
Dividends	210

(1) Jackie's total non-savings income for 2016/17 is:

£	

(2) Jackie's total savings income for 2016/17 is:

£	

(3) Jackie's total dividend income for 2016/17 is:

£	

(b) Sandy works for Geese Ltd. She is paid monthly and has an annual salary of £54,000. In March 2017 she received a bonus of £10,000.

Sandy's Class 1 Primary national insurance contributions for 2016/17 were (tick ONE):

	✓
£6,712	
£4,612	
£4,600	
£5,580	

Task 8

Mr and Mrs Shah are thinking of buying a property to rent out. Mrs Shah is a stay at home mum with no income and Mr Shah is a higher rate taxpayer. Mrs Shah has savings in an ISA that she accumulated whilst she was working full time.

Suggest ways in which Mr and Mrs Shah could arrange this purchase in order to save tax for them as a couple.

This style of task would be human marked in the exam.

Task 9

(a) Classify whether a disposal of each of the following assets will be chargeable to or exempt from capital gains tax:

Asset	Chargeable	Exempt
Shares in XYZ plc held in an ISA		
Ruby necklace valued at £100,000		
Vintage Rolls Royce Car		
Factory used in a trade		

(b) Trevor bought a 5 acre plot of land for £50,000. He sold 3 acres of the land at auction for £105,000 in August 2016. He had spent £2,500 installing drainage on the 3 acres which he sold. His disposal costs were £1,500. The market value of the remaining 2 acres at the date of sale was £45,000.

The gain on sale of the 3 acres is:

	✓
£66,000	
£66,750	
£71,000	
£66,152	

(c) **(1)** Matt bought a picture for £7,000 and had costs of acquisition of £300. He sold it in August 2016 for £4,500 and had costs of disposal of £200.

The allowable loss on sale is: (either show the loss by using brackets or a minus sign)

£	

(2) Keith bought a greyhound for £5,000. It won a number of races and he sold it for £7,000 in December 2016, incurring costs of disposal of £250.

The chargeable gain on sale is:

	✓
Nil	
£1,667	
£1,250	
£1,750	

Task 10

Lee had the following transactions in shares in Snowy Ltd:

Acquisitions	No of shares	Cost £
December 2006	10,000	10,800
August 2007	Bonus, 1 for 1	Nil
June 2011	10,000	8,700
December 2011	Rights Issue, 1 for 10	40p each

Disposal		Proceeds £
September 2016	15,000	18,650

Using the proforma layout provided, calculate the chargeable gain made on the disposal of the shares in Snowy Ltd, and show the balance of shares to be carried forward for future disposal. Fill in all unshaded boxes, enter 0 if appropriate. Both brackets and minus signs can be used to show negative numbers.

Gain

	£
Proceeds of sale	
Less cost	
Chargeable gain	

Share pool

	No of shares	Cost £
December 2006 Acquisition		
August 2007 Bonus issue		
June 2011 Acquisition		
December 2011 Rights issue		
September 2016 Disposal		
c/f		

Task 11

Irma had the following chargeable gains in 2016/17:

Gain on sale of shares August 2016	£9,341
Gain on sale of furniture February 2017	£4,167
She had allowable losses brought forward of	£1,000

Irma is an additional rate taxpayer.

(a) Irma's taxable gains for 2016/17 are:

£	

(b) Irma's CGT payable for 2016/17 is:

£	

(c) Irma's CGT is due for payment by: (enter date as xx/xx/xxxx)

£	

Task 12

(a) Gillian owned a 70% shareholding in R Ltd, an unquoted investment company. On 23 July 2016, she gave a 20% shareholding in R Ltd to her son. The values of shareholdings in R Ltd on 23 July 2016 were as follows:

	£
100% shareholding	600,000
70% shareholding	350,000
50% shareholding	200,000
20% shareholding	80,000

What is the diminution in value of Gillian's estate as a result of her gift on 23 July 2016?

	✓
£150,000	
£270,000	
£80,000	
£120,000	

(b) Joel and Sunita were a married couple. Sunita died in July 2008 and 65% of her nil rate band of £312,000 (2008/09) was unused. Joel died in May 2016. He had made a potentially exempt transfer (after all available exemptions) of £75,000 in August 2011. Joel left his estate to his sister. Any relevant elections were made.

What is the nil rate band available to set against Joel's death estate?

	✓
£325,000	
£452,800	
£461,250	
£536,250	

Task 13

(a) Mary made the following gifts in the tax year 2016/17:

(1) £1,000 on the first day of each month for nine months to her niece to pay university living expenses. Mary used income surplus to her living requirements to make these payments.

(2) £200 to her grandson on his birthday and a further £250 to the same grandson as a Christmas gift.

Ignoring the annual exemption, what is the total value of potentially exempt transfers made by Mary as a result of these gifts?

	✓
£9,350	
£100	
£9,000	
£450	

(b) Georgia owns the following assets:

(1) A property valued at £674,000 with an outstanding mortgage of £160,000.

(2) Vintage motor cars valued at £172,000.

(3) Investments in Individual Savings Accounts valued at £47,000.

Georgia owes £22,400 in respect of a personal loan from a bank, and she has also verbally promised to pay legal fees of £4,600 incurred by her nephew. Her reasonable funeral expenses will amount to £5,500.

Georgia's husband died on 12 March 2009, and 70% of his inheritance tax nil rate band was not used.

Georgia has only made one lifetime gift of £100,000 in March 2015 to her son.

Calculate the inheritance tax due as a result of Georgia's death in 2016/17.

This style of task would be human marked in the exam.

BPP PRACTICE ASSESSMENT 2 PERSONAL TAX

ANSWERS

Personal Tax (PLTX)
BPP practice assessment 2

Task 1

(a) **(1)** The scale charge percentage for the first car is:

22	**%**

110g/km – 95g/km = 15/5 = 3% + 16% + 3%

(2) The taxable benefit for the first car is:

£	1,771

£13,800 × 22% × 7/12

(3) The scale charge percentage for the second car is:

15	**%**

(Between 76g/km and 94g/km)

(4) The taxable benefit for the second car is:

£	750

£12,000 × 15% × 5/12

(5) The fuel benefit for the second car is:

£	1,388

£22,200 × 15% × 5/12

(b) Professional competence and due care

(c) Confidentiality

Task 2

(a)

	✓
Long service award of £900 to employee with 30 years of service	
Workplace parking	
Workplace childcare facilities	
Moving expenses of £10,000	✓

Moving expenses of £10,000 are only exempt up to £8,000, the excess is taxable.

The long service award is wholly exempt as it is within the limit of £50 for each year of service and the period of service is in excess of 20 years.

(b) **(1)** The taxable benefit for 2016/17 is:

£	0

No taxable benefit arises if the combined outstanding balance on all loans to the employee did not exceed £10,000 at any time in the tax year.

(2) The taxable benefit for 2016/17 is:

£	0

Exempt

(c) **(1)** The basic accommodation benefit for 2016/17 is:

£	600

	£
Annual value	1,500
Less payment by employee £75 × 12 =	(900)
Basic accommodation benefit	600

(2) The cost of providing the accommodation for calculating the additional benefit is:

£	125,000

Market value at provision (acquired more than 6 years before provision)

(3) The additional accommodation benefit for 2016/17 is:

£	1,500

Excess of £125,000 over £75,000 = £50,000 × 3%

(4) The benefit for provision of furniture for 2016/17 is:

£	3,000

£15,000 × 20%

Task 3

(a) The salary to be included in employment income for 2016/17 is:

£	36,180

	£
Salary April to December 2016 9/12 × £36,000	27,000
Salary January to March 2017 3/12 × £(36,000 × 102%)	9,180

(b) The bonus to be included in employment income for 2016/17 is:

£	2,000

Bonus received 31 March 2017

(c) The commission to be included in employment income for 2016/17 is:

£	0

Commission received 30 April 2017 (taxable in 2017/18)

(d) The benefit to be included in employment income for 2016/17 is:

£	0

Exempt benefit

Task 4

(a) **(1)** The amount of the dividend not taxed at 0% is:

£	2,500

£7,500 – £5,000

(2) The tax rate applicable to the amount in (1) is:

32.5	%

She is a higher rate taxpayer

(3) The income tax payable on the dividend income is (to the nearest £1)

£	813

£2,500 × 32.5%

(b) **(1)** His personal savings allowance is:

£	1,000

Paul is a basic rate taxpayer

(2) His taxable savings income after the savings allowance is:

£	2,500

ISA interest is exempt. BSI £3,500 – £1,000 = £2,500

(3) The income tax payable on his savings income for 2016/17 is:

£	500

£2,500 × 20% = £500

Task 5

(a)

	Property 1 £	Property 2 £
Rental income		
Property 1 £12,000 × 7/12	7,000	
Property 2 £9,000 × 8/12		6,000
Less expenses		
Insurance £700/£800 × 9/12	(525)	(600)
Accountancy	(100)	0
Repainting	(400)	0
Redecoration	0	(900)
Replacement carpets and curtains	0	(600)
Net income	5,975	3,900
Total property income 2016/17	9,875	

(b)

	✓
A new fridge to replace the one that stopped working last week	✓
A television for the new conservatory	
New carpet for the living room after the old one was damaged in the recent floods	✓
New crockery for the kitchen to replace the chipped plates and bowls	✓

The television is not a replacement as the conservatory is new and therefore there would not have been one there before.

Task 6

(a) **(1)** Non-savings income:

£	54,678

	£
£32,000 × 20%	6,400
£118,000 × 40%	47,200
£2,395 × 45%	1,078
£152,395	54,678

(2) Savings income:

£	65

£145 × 45% (Additional rate taxpayers do not get a personal savings allowance)

(3) Dividend income:

£	0

This is covered by the dividend allowance.

(4) Donald's tax payable for 2016/17 is:

£	2,743

	£
Income tax liability £(54,678 + 65 + 0)	54,743
PAYE	(52,000)
Income tax payable	2,743

(b)

From: AATStudent@boxmail.net
To: SMiles@webmail.net
Sent: 1 December 2017
Subject: Pensions

Occupational pension schemes operate by the employer deducting your pension contribution from your salary before the PAYE is calculated. In your case this would be 5%. This means that full tax relief is automatically obtained at source at your applicable rate of tax. The employer is responsible for paying over the pension payments to the pension provider.

The 7% that your employer pays to the pension scheme on your behalf has no tax implications for you, ie this will not be classed as a taxable benefit.

Private pension schemes work quite differently. You pay the pension provider direct, usually monthly. The amount you pay is net of basic rate tax.

So if for example, you decide you would like to put £100 a month into your pension, you only actually have to pay in £80, HM Revenue & Customs will pay the other £20. This automatically provides you with 20% tax relief.

If however, you are a higher or additional rate taxpayer, you will be entitled to further tax relief. In order to get tax relief at the higher rate of 40% or the additional rate of 45%, the basic rate band (and also the additional rate threshold) is extended by the gross pension contributions so that the 40% and 45% tax rates will apply after the pension has been adjusted for.

Task 7

(a) **(1)** Jackie's total non-savings income for 2016/17 is:

£	25,000

£20,000 + £5,000

(2) Jackie's total savings income for 2016/17 is:

£	325

£145 + £180 = £325

(3) Jackie's total dividend income for 2016/17 is:

£	210

Dividends from ISAs are exempt.

(b) Sandy's Class 1 Primary national insurance contributions for 2016/17 were:

	✓
£6,712	
£4,612	
£4,600	✓
£5,580	

Workings:

£(54,000/12) = £4,500 per month

£(3,583 – 672) = 2,911 × 12% × 11 months =	3,843
£(4,500 – 3,583) = 917 × 2% × 11 months =	202
£(3,583 – 672) = 2,911 × 12% × 1 month =	349
£(14,500 – 3,583) = 10,917 × 2% × 1 month =	218
	£4,612

Task 8

As Mrs Shah has savings but no income at present she is not paying any tax. Any interest she receives from her ISA is exempt from Income Tax.

Mr Shah is a higher rate tax payer who would pay 40% income tax on any rents received.

The rental income would be allocated between them based on their percentage ownership.

Mr and Mrs Shah should arrange the purchase so that Mrs Shah receives as much rent as possible so that she uses her personal allowance. Any income above her personal allowance would be taxed at 20%.

This would mean that the first £11,000 of the income would not be taxable as it would be covered by her personal allowance and anything above that would be taxed at 20% in her hands as opposed to 40% if Mr Shah received it.

Task 9

(a)

Asset	Chargeable	Exempt
Shares in XYZ plc held in an ISA		✓
Ruby necklace valued at £100,000	✓	
Vintage Rolls Royce Car		✓
Factory used in a trade	✓	

(b)

	✓
£66,000	✓
£66,750	
£71,000	
£66,152	

	£
Proceeds of sale	105,000
Less costs of disposal	(1,500)
Net proceeds	103,500
Less cost	
(105,000/105,000 + 45,000) × £50,000	(35,000)
enhancement expenditure	(2,500)
Chargeable gain	66,000

(c) **(1)** The allowable loss on sale is:

£	(1,500)

	£
Deemed disposal proceeds	6,000
Less costs of disposal	(200)
Net deemed disposal proceeds	5,800
Less cost £(7,000 + 300)	(7,300)
Allowable loss	(1,500)

(2)

	✓
Nil	✓
£1,667	
£1,250	
£1,750	

The greyhound is a wasting chattel and so is an exempt asset. Therefore there is no chargeable gain on the disposal.

Task 10

Gain

	£
Proceeds of sale	18,650
Less cost	(9,409)
Chargeable gain	9,241

Share pool

	No of shares	Cost £
December 2006 Acquisition	10,000	10,800
August 2007 Bonus 1 for 1	10,000	0
	20,000	10,800
June 2011 Acquisition	10,000	8,700
	30,000	19,500
December 2011 Rights 1 for 10 × £0.40	3,000	1,200
	33,000	20,700
September 2016 Disposal (15,000/33,000 × £20,700)	(15,000)	(9,409)
c/f	18,000	11,291

Task 11

(a) Irma's taxable gains for 2016/17 are:

£	1,408

	£
Gain on shares	9,341
Gain on furniture	4,167
	13,508
Less loss brought forward	(1,000)
Net chargeable gains	12,508
Less annual exempt amount	(11,100)
Taxable gains	1,408

(b) Irma's CGT payable for 2016/17 is:

£	282

£1,408 × 20%

(c) Irma's CGT is due for payment by:

31/01/2018

Task 12

(a)

	✓
£150,000	✓
£270,000	
£80,000	
£120,000	

Workings:

	£
Before the gift: 70% shareholding	350,000
After the gift: 50% shareholding	(200,000)
Transfer of value	150,000

(b)

	✓
£325,000	
£452,800	
£461,250	✓
£536,250	

Workings:

	£
Sunita's unused nil rate band £325,000 × 65%	211,250
Joel's nil rate band	325,000
	536,250
Less used against Joel's PET now chargeable	(75,000)
Available nil rate band to set against Joel's death estate	461,250

Task 13

(a)

	✓
£9,350	
£100	
£9,000	
£450	✓

Workings:

The gifts to the niece are exempt as normal expenditure out of income because they are part of the normal expenditure of the donor, made out of income and left the donor with sufficient income to maintain her usual standard of living.

The small gifts exemption only applies to gifts up to £250 per donee per tax year. If gifts total more than £250 the whole amount is chargeable. Since the gifts to the grandson totalled £(200 + 250) = £450 in 2016/17, this exemption does not apply.

(b) Inheritance tax due:

Death estate:

	£
Property	674,000
Less repayment mortgage	(160,000)
	514,000
Motor cars	172,000
Investments	47,000
Bank loan	(22,400)
Nephew's legal fees *	(0)
Funeral expenses	(5,500)
	705,100
Tax:	
Nil band: £458,500** × 0%	0
£246,600 × 40%	98,640
Total IHT due	98,640

* The promise to pay the nephew's legal fees is not deductible as it is purely gratuitous (not made for valuable consideration).

** Georgia's nil band: £(325,000 – 94,000 PET less 2xAE's)	231,000
Unused nil band of husband: £(325,000 × 70%)	227,500

BPP PRACTICE ASSESSMENT 3
PERSONAL TAX

Time allowed: 2.5 hours

PRACTICE ASSESSMENT 3

Personal Tax (PLTX)
BPP practice assessment 3

Task 1

(a) Khalid works for KML plc, and is provided with a company car for business and private use from 6 June 2016.

The car has a diesel engine with CO_2 emissions of 152g/km. It has a list price of £27,000, although the company actually paid £23,500 for the car. Khalid agreed to make a capital contribution of £6,000 towards the cost of the car. The company pays for all running costs, including all fuel. Khalid pays £50 a month towards the cost of private fuel – the actual cost of private fuel is about £90 a month.

(1) The cost of the car in the taxable benefit computation is:

	✓
£21,000	
£22,000	
£17,500	
£18,500	

(2) The percentage used in the taxable benefit computation is:

	%

(3) The taxable benefit in respect of the provision of fuel for private use is:

£	

(b) What category of national insurance would be payable on this benefit, who is liable for this National Insurance and how much is the national insurance contribution?

(1) Category of National Insurance

[▼]

(2) Who is liable for this National Insurance?

[▼]

(3) How much is the national insurance contribution? State your answer to the nearest £1.

£	

Picklist for questions (b) (1) and (2)

Class 1 Primary
Class 1 Secondary
Class 1 A
Employee
Employer

Task 2

(a) Lou is employed by Jane Quentin and receives the following benefits as a result of her employment.

In each case enter the taxable benefit arising. Enter 0 if the benefit is not taxable.

(1) An interest free loan of £10,500 made on 1 July 2016, no repayments made during 2016/17.

£	

(2) Cash voucher for £100 provided in December 2016. Jane acquired the voucher for £90.

£	

(3) Van for business and private use from 1 October 2016 onwards.

£	

(4) Fuel for van for private use from 1 January 2017 onwards.

£	

(b) For each of the following benefits, tick whether they would be partly exempt or wholly exempt if received by an employee who is a basic rate taxpayer in 2016/17:

Benefit	Partly exempt	Wholly exempt
Staff party costing £125 per head		
Childcare vouchers of £55 per week		
Removal expenses of £10,000		
Work related training costing £1,500		

(c) Madge is employed by V plc. She uses her own car for business purposes and is reimbursed 45p per mile by her employer. Madge travelled 15,000 miles on business in 2016/17.

What are the employment income consequences of the reimbursement for business mileage?

	✓
£6,750 taxable benefit	
£1,000 taxable benefit	
No taxable benefit or allowable deduction	
£1,000 allowable deduction	

Task 3

(a) The following amounts were received in relation to employment:

(1) Monthly salary of £1,500 paid on the last working day of each month

(2) Tips of £300 paid by customers directly to an employee

(3) Employer's contribution of 6% of salary to company's occupational pension scheme

(4) Reimbursement of business expenses of £500

For each item, tick either taxable or not taxable:

Item	Taxable	Not taxable
Salary		
Tips		
Employer's pension contribution		
Reimbursement of business expenses		

(b) Eric Wright was born in September 1959 and is employed as an architect. His employment income for 2016/17 was £96,870 and PAYE of £28,500 was deducted at source.

Eric has a bank account with the Halifax Bank. His account was credited with interest of £2,000 on 31 March 2017.

Eric received a dividend of £7,500 on 1 July 2016.

Eric made a Gift Aid donation of £400 to Oxfam on 1 December 2016.

Using the proforma layout provided, prepare a schedule of Eric's taxable income for 2016/17, clearly showing the distinction between non-savings, savings and dividend income. Both brackets and minus signs can be used to show negative numbers.

	Non-savings income £	Savings income £	Dividend income £	Total £

Task 4

(a) A higher rate taxpayer receives £3,250 of bank interest, £250 of which was from his cash ISA, and £10,000 of dividends during 2016/17. What amounts will be liable to income tax at a rate of above 0% in 2016/17?

	✓
£3,000 of interest and £5,000 of dividends	
£3,000 of interest and £10,000 of dividends	
£2,250 of interest and £5,000 of dividends	
£2,500 of interest and £5,000 of dividends	

(b) Tick the relevant box to show which of the following types of income are chargeable to income tax and which are exempt from income tax:

Source of income	Chargeable	Exempt
Individual Savings Account interest		
Government stock interest		
Dividends received from an Individual Savings Account		
Bank deposit account interest		

Task 5

(a) Michaela rents out a house from 1 July 2016.

She charges a rent of £600 per month payable in arrears on the last day of each month. The tenants don't pay the rent due on 31 March 2017 until 10 April 2017.

Michaela also pays an insurance premium of £400 on 6 July 2016, covering the period 6 July 2016 to 5 July 2017.

(1) The rental income taxable for 2016/17 is:

£	

(2) The insurance premium allowable as an expense for 2016/17 is:

£	

(b) Wilma owns two flats that she rents out. Flat A is unfurnished. Flat B is furnished.

The income and expenses for these properties are:

	Flat A £	Flat B £
Monthly income:		
Rent	500	650
Annual expenses:		
Council tax	1,000	800
Water rates	300	300
Insurance	350	250

Flat A was fully occupied during 2016/17. However, the tenants in Flat B moved out in November 2016 having paid the rent to the end of that month. Wilma was unable to re-let the flat until June 2017.

Wilma spent £410 replacing various items of furniture for Flat B that had been damaged by the outgoing tenants.

Wilma had a loss of £1,200 on her income from property in 2015/16.

Using the proforma layout below, calculate Wilma's property income for 2016/17. Fill in all unshaded boxes, enter 0 if appropriate. Both brackets and minus signs can be used to show negative numbers.

	Flat A £	Flat B £
Income		
Expenses:		
Council tax		
Water rates		
Insurance		
Replacement furniture relief		
Net income from property		
Total property income		
Less loss b/f		
Taxable property income		

Task 6

(a) Guy has the following income for 2016/17:

	£
Employment income (PAYE £250)	11,650
Interest received from building societies	46,250
Dividends received	14,000

Calculate Guy's income tax payable for 2016/17 entering your answer and workings into the blank table below. Brackets or a minus sign are both acceptable when entering negative numbers.

(b) Guy is considering asking his employer to set up a small charitable donation of about £50 a month and deduct it out of his salary, but is unsure if he will get any tax relief for this.

Explain to Guy how he will get tax relief on such donations.

Task 7

You receive the following email from a client, who is a higher rate taxpayer.

From:	Raman99@sherbet.net
To:	AATStudent@boxmail.net
Sent:	20 June 2017
Subject:	More information

Hello, I am so sorry, I know that you have already sent in my tax form for 2016/17. Unfortunately, I have forgotten to tell you that I started letting out a property on 1 January 2017 and received £3,000 of rental income for the first three months.

I suggest we leave the 2016/17 return as it is and I will just account for the income as if I started renting the property in April 2017.

Thanks.

Raman

Reply to Raman's email.

From:	AATStudent@boxmail.net
To:	Raman99@sherbet.net
Sent:	22 June 2017
Subject:	More information

Task 8

Owen is employed by X Ltd throughout 2016/17. He earns £55,000 a year. He also receives interest income from a Santander Bank current account.

Owen could do the following to save tax:

	True	False
Invest his savings in an ISA		
Donate to charity under the Gift Aid scheme		
Invest in a property		
Contribute to a pension		
Invest in a tax avoidance scheme set up by his friend		

Task 9

(a) For each statement, tick the appropriate box in respect of the capital gains calculation.

Disposal	Market value used	Actual proceeds used	No gain/no loss disposal
Olivia sells shares for £5,000 to her wife Lucy when they are worth £4,000			
William sells land to his brother for £10,000 when it is worth £50,000			
Zeta gives an asset worth £4,000 to her friend Tanya			
Olwyn sells listed shares for proceeds of £12,000			

(b) Melly bought a holiday cottage for £32,000, incurring legal costs of £600 on the purchase. She spent £6,000 on adding a conservatory to the cottage. This was destroyed during a storm in 2013 and not replaced. Melly sold the cottage in March 2017 for £45,000. She paid estate agent's fees of £900 and legal costs of £350.

The chargeable gain on sale is:

£	

(c) **(1)** Suki purchased a vase for £9,500. In December 2016 she sold the vase at auction for £2,500. This amount is before deducting the auctioneer's 10% commission.

The allowable loss on sale is:

	✓
£3,750	
£3,500	
£7,000	
£7,250	

(2) **A chattel with a useful life of 60 years or less is a wasting chattel.**

	✓
True	
False	

Task 10

Vernon sold 4,000 shares in R Ltd for £36,200 on 23 February 2017. He had acquired his holdings in R Ltd as follows:

Date	Transaction	No of shares	£
14 April 2001	Purchase	6,000	18,400
29 May 2006	Rights issue	1 for 20	£4 each
10 March 2017	Purchase	500	3,400

Using the proforma layout provided, compute the total gain on sale. Both brackets and minus signs can be used to show negative numbers.

Share pool

	No of shares	Cost £

Total gain on sale

	£

Task 11

(a) Desmond bought a house in Glasgow on 1 April 2002. He lived in the house until 30 September 2005. He was then sent to work in Bristol by his employer, before returning to live in the house again on 1 October 2010. He lived in the house before moving out on 30 April 2011 to live with friends until the house was sold on 30 September 2016.

Using the proforma layout provided, show which periods of ownership are exempt and which are chargeable matching the correct explanation for each period.

Explanation	Exempt (dates)	Chargeable (dates)
▼	▼	▼
▼	▼	▼
▼	▼	▼
▼	▼	▼
▼	▼	▼
▼	▼	▼

Picklist for explanation:	Picklist for dates:
Not occupied and not followed by actual occupation	1 October 2005 to 30 September 2009
Actual occupation	1 May 2011 to 31 March 2015
Actual occupation	1 April 2002 to 30 September 2005
Last 18 months ownership	1 October 2009 to 30 September 2010
Up to three years any reason	1 April 2015 to 30 September 2016
Four years employed elsewhere in UK	1 October 2010 to 30 April 2011

(b) Desmond purchased the property for £210,000 on 1 April 2002, and received disposal proceeds of £385,000 on 30 September 2016. It is his main residence.

After applying principal private residence relief, the sale of Desmond's house will result in a chargeable gain.

	✓
True	
False	

(c) **If any capital gains tax is payable on the sale of his house, by what date must Desmond pay this? (xx/xx/xxxx)**

Task 12

(a) Rodney died on 13 August 2016. In his will he left £200 in cash to each of his five nephews, investments held in ISAs valued at £350,000 to his daughter, and the residue of his estate, which amounted to £520,000, to his wife.

What is the chargeable estate for inheritance purposes?

£	

(b) Kirstin gave shares worth £150,000 to a trust on 15 September 2007 and shares worth £600,000 to her brother on 10 July 2013. Kirstin died on 23 October 2016.

Ignoring the annual exemption, what is the inheritance tax payable on Kirstin's death in relation to her lifetime transfers? (Assume the nil band has always been £325,000)

	✓
£170,000	
£88,000	
£136,000	
£132,160	

Task 13

Jimmy died on 14 February 2017. He had used up his nil rate band at the date of his death by making the following gifts during his lifetime:

(1) On 2 August 2015 Jimmy made a cash gift to his grandson as a wedding gift when he got married.

(2) On 9 September 2015 Jimmy gave 200 shares valued at £5 each in J Ltd, an unquoted investment company, to his daughter. Before the gift, Jimmy owned 5,100 shares valued at £30 each in J Ltd. After the gift Jimmy owned 4,900 shares valued at £20 each in J Ltd.

(3) On 14 November 2015 Jimmy made a cash gift of £800,000 to a trust. Jimmy paid the inheritance tax arising from this gift.

(a) What was the total amount of the exemptions that were deducted in computing the potentially exempt transfer made on 2 August 2015?

	✓
£3,000	
£8,500	
£6,000	
£11,000	

(b) What is the diminution in value in Jimmy's estate as a result of his gift on 9 September 2015 ?

	✓
£55,000	
£4,000	
£6,000	
£1,000	

(c) What was the amount of the inheritance tax paid by Jimmy as a result of his gift made on 14 November 2015?

£	

BPP PRACTICE ASSESSMENT 3 PERSONAL TAX

ANSWERS

Personal Tax (PLTX)
BPP practice assessment 3

Task 1

(a) **(1)** The cost of the car in the taxable benefit computation is:

	✓
£21,000	
£22,000	✓
£17,500	
£18,500	

List price £27,000 less capital contribution paid by employee (max) £5,000

(2) The percentage used in the taxable benefit computation is:

30	%

150 – 95 = 55
55 ÷ 5 = 11%
16% + 11% + 3% (diesel) = 30%

(3) The taxable benefit in respect of the provision of fuel for private use is:

£	5,550

£22,200 × 30% × 10/12 (There is no reduction for part reimbursement of private fuel).

(b) **(1)** Category of national insurance

Class 1A

(2) Who is liable for this national insurance?

Employer

(3) How much is the national insurance contribution? State your answer to the nearest £1.

£	766

£5,550 (from part (3)) × 13.8%

Task 2

(a) **(1)**

£	236

£10,500 × 3% × 9/12

(2)

£	100

(3)

£	1,585

£3,170 × 6/12

(4)

£	150

£598 × 3/12

(b)

Benefit	Partly exempt	Wholly exempt
Staff party costing £125 per head		✓
Childcare vouchers of £55 per week		✓
Removal expenses of £10,000	✓ (up to £8,000)	
Work related training costing £1,500		✓

(c)

	✓
£6,750 taxable benefit	
£1,000 taxable benefit	✓
No taxable benefit or allowable deduction	
£1,000 allowable deduction	

	£
Amount reimbursed 15,000 × 45p	6,750
Less statutory allowance	
10,000 miles × 45p	(4,500)
5,000 miles × 25p	(1,250)
Taxable benefit	1,000

Task 3

(a)

Item	Taxable	Not taxable
Salary	✓	
Tips	✓	
Employer's pension contribution		✓
Reimbursement of business expenses		✓

(b)

	Non-savings income £	Savings income £	Dividend income £	Total £
Employment income	96,870			
Bank interest		2,000		
Dividends			7,500	
Net income	96,870	2,000	7,500	106,370
Less personal allowance	(8,065)			(8,065)
Taxable income	88,805	2,000	7,500	98,305

Workings:

	£
Personal allowance	11,000
Less half excess (see below)	(2,935)
	8,065
Total net income	106,370
Adjustment for Gift Aid donation £400 × 100/80	(500)
Adjusted net income	105,870
Less income limit	(100,000)
Excess	5,870

Task 4

(a)

	✓
£3,000 of interest and £5,000 of dividends	
£3,000 of interest and £10,000 of dividends	
£2,250 of interest and £5,000 of dividends	
£2,500 of interest and £5,000 of dividends	✓

The taxable interest is after deduction of the savings allowance (£500 for higher rate tax payers) and excludes the ISA interest. £3,250 – £250 – £500 = £2,500. The first £5,000 of dividends are taxable at 0% for all taxpayers.

(b)

Source of income	Chargeable	Exempt
Individual Savings Account interest		✓
Government stock interest	✓	
Dividends received from an Individual Savings Account		✓
Bank deposit account interest	✓	

Task 5

(a) **(1)** The rental income taxable for 2016/17 is:

£	5,400

Rental income accrued 2016/17:

1 July 2016 to 31 March 2017 (working in whole months)

9 months × £600 per month

The actual date of receipt of the rent due on 31 March 2017 is not relevant.

(2) The insurance premium allowable as an expense for 2016/17 is:

£	300

£400 × 9/12

(b)

	Flat A £	Flat B £
Income: £500 × 12/ £650 × 8	6,000	5,200
Expenses:		
Council tax	(1,000)	(800)
Water rates	(300)	(300)
Insurance	(350)	(250)
Replacement furniture relief	(0)	(410)
Net income from property	4,350	3,440
Total property income £(4,350 + 3,440)	7,790	
Less loss b/f	(1,200)	
Taxable property income	6,590	

Task 6

(a)

	Non savings income £	Savings income £	Dividend income £
Employment income	11,650		
Building society interest		46,250	
Dividends			14,000
Personal allowance	(11,000)		
Taxable income	650	46,250	14,000
Income tax			
£650 × 20%			130
£500 x 0% (savings allowance)			0
£4,350 (£5,000 – £650) × 0%			0
£26,500 (£32,000 – £650 – £500 – £4,350) × 20%			5,300
£14,900 (£46,250 – £500 – £4,350 – £26,500) × 40%			5,960
£5,000 × 0%			0
£9,000 × 32.5%			2,925
Income tax liability			14,315
Less tax deducted at source:			
PAYE			(250)
Income tax payable			14,065

(b)

Guy's employer will deduct the donation from his salary before it is taxed. If he decides to pay £50 a month, this will mean he will get tax relief during the year on £600 (£50 × 12). This will reduce his taxable employment income to £50.

Note. You would not be expected to recalculate the tax here but for information the calculation would be as follows:

Income tax	
£50 × 20%	10
£500 × 0%	0
£4,950 (£5,000 – £50) × 0%	0
£26,500 (£32,000 – £4,950 – 50 – 500) × 20%	5,300
£14,300 (£46,250 – £26,500 – £500 – £4,950) × 40%	5,720
£5,000 × 0% + £9,000 × 32.5% (as above)	2,925
Income tax liability	13,955

Tax saving £14,315 – £13,955 = £360

This seems a large saving on a £600 reduction in income (60%!) but can be explained:

£600 employment income which would have been taxed at 20% is not taxed at all saving £120.

An extra £600 of the starting rate band is available meaning that income that would have been taxed at 20% is now taxed at 0% saving £120.

£600 of savings income is now taxed at 20% rather than 40% saving another £120.

Task 7

From:	AATStudent@boxmail.net
To:	Raman99@sherbet.net
Sent:	22 June 2017
Subject:	More information

Thank you for your email. Unfortunately I cannot condone the action you have suggested as it amounts to tax evasion. By not declaring the income you are deliberately misleading HMRC resulting in an underpayment of your tax in 2016/17. Should they choose to look into your tax return and discover this omission you would be liable to interest and penalties.

Ultimately it is your choice and I can only advise you as to the correct course of action. However, if you choose not to take my advice then I would have to cease acting for you with regard to your tax affairs and inform HMRC that I have done so. I will not tell them why as this would be a breach of client confidentiality.

I hope it doesn't come to this. Please feel free to contact me to discuss this matter further.

Task 8

	True	False
Invest his savings in an ISA	✓	
Donate to charity under the Gift Aid scheme	✓	
Invest in a property		✓
Contribute to a pension	✓	
Invest in a tax avoidance scheme set up by his friend		✓**

*Investing in a property would not save tax as the rental income would be taxable as non-savings income.

**Investing in a tax avoidance scheme is risky and whilst it may save tax initially it could end up not saving tax if HMRC decide to close down the scheme.

Task 9

(a)

Disposal	Market value used	Actual proceeds used	No gain/no loss disposal
Olivia sells shares for £5,000 to her wife Lucy when they are worth £4,000			✓
William sells land to his brother for £10,000 when it is worth £50,000	✓		
Zeta gives an asset worth £4,000 to her friend Tanya	✓		
Olwyn sells listed shares for proceeds of £12,000		✓	

(b) The chargeable gain on sale is:

£	11,150

	£
Proceeds of sale	45,000
Less disposal costs £(900 + 350)	(1,250)
Net proceeds of sale	43,750
Less costs of acquisition £(32,000 + 600)	(32,600)
enhancement expenditure (not reflected in value of property on disposal)	(Nil)
Chargeable gain	11,150

(c) **(1)** The allowable loss on sale is:

	✓
£3,750	✓
£3,500	
£7,000	
£7,250	

	£
Deemed proceeds of sale	6,000
Less disposal costs (10% × £2,500)	(250)
Net proceeds of sale	5,750
Less cost	(9,500)
Allowable loss	(3,750)

(2) A chattel with a useful life of 60 years or less is a wasting chattel.

	✓
True	
False	✓

A chattel with a useful life of 50 years or less is a wasting chattel.

Task 10

Share pool

	No of shares	Cost £
14.4.01 Acquisition	6,000	18,400
29.5.06 Rights 1 for 20 × £4 (1/20 × 6,000)	300	1,200
	6,300	19,600
23.2.17 Disposal (3,500/6,300 × £19,600)	(3,500)	(10,889)
c/f	2,800	8,711

Total gain on sale

	£
First match with acquisitions in the next 30 days:	
Proceeds of sale $\frac{500}{4,000} \times$ £36,200	4,525
Less allowable cost	(3,400)
Gain	1,125
Next match with shares in the share pool:	
Proceeds of sale $\frac{3,500}{4,000} \times$ £36,200	31,675
Less allowable cost (from share pool above)	(10,889)
Gain	20,786
Total gains (£1,125 + £20,786)	21,911

Task 11

(a)

Explanation	Exempt (dates)	Chargeable (dates)
Actual occupation	1 April 2002 to 30 September 2005	
Four years employed elsewhere in UK	1 October 2005 to30 September 2009	
Up to three years any reason	1 October 2009 to30 September 2010	
Actual occupation	1 October 2010 to30 September 2011	
Not occupied and not followed by actual occupation		1 May 2011 to 31 March 2015
Last 18 months ownership	1 April 2015 to 30 September 2016	

(b)

	✓
True	✓
False	

(c) Capital gains tax for 2016/17 is payable by:

31/01/2018

Task 12

(a) The chargeable estate for inheritance purposes is:

£	351,000

	£
Cash to nephews £200 × 5	1,000
ISA investments	350,000
Chargeable estate	351,000

The small gifts exemption only applies to lifetime transfers. The ISA exemption only applies for income tax and capital gains tax. The residue to the wife is covered by the spouse exemption.

(b)

	✓
£170,000	
£88,000	
£136,000	✓
£132,160	

10.7.13 PET now chargeable	600,000
Less nil rate band available £(£325,000 – 150,000)	(175,000)
	425,000
IHT @ 40%	170,000
Less taper relief (3 to 4 years) @ 20%	(34,000)
Death tax payable on lifetime transfer	136,000

The chargeable lifetime transfer on 15 September 2007 is cumulated with the later PET since it was made in the seven years before that transfer.

Task 13

(a)

	✓
£3,000	
£8,500	✓
£6,000	
£11,000	

	£
Marriage exemption (remoter ancestor)	2,500
Annual exemption 2015/16	3,000
Annual exemption 2014/15 b/f	3,000
	8,500

(b)

	✓
£55,000	✓
£4,000	
£6,000	
£1,000	

	£
Before the gift: 5,100 shares × £30	153,000
After the gift: 4,900 shares × £20	(98,000)
Diminution in value	55,000

(c)

£	118,750

	£
Net transfer of value (Jimmy pays IHT)	800,000
IHT £325,000 × 0% =	Nil
£475,000 × 20/80 =	118,750
£800,000	118,750

BPP PRACTICE ASSESSMENT 4
PERSONAL TAX

Time allowed: 2.5 hours

PRACTICE ASSESSMENT 4

Personal Tax (PLTX)
BPP practice assessment 4

Task 1

In October 2014 her employer provided Antonia with a second-hand Ford Focus car. It cost the company £14,000, but the list price of this car when bought new was £21,000. The car has a CO_2 emission of 90g/km, and has a petrol engine. The company sold the Ford Focus on 31 December 2016 and immediately provided Antonia with a brand new Volvo car. The Volvo has a list price of £27,000, but Antonia had to make a capital contribution of £6,500 towards it. The car has a CO_2 emission of 170g/km and has a diesel engine.

The company pays for all running costs for both cars including the fuel. Antonia pays £80 per month to the company as part of the cost of fuel used privately.

(a) The cost of the Ford Focus in the taxable benefit computation is:

£	

(b) The taxable benefit in respect of the provision of the Ford Focus for private use in 2016/17 is:

£	

(c) The taxable benefit in respect of the provision of fuel for the Ford Focus for private use in 2016/17 is:

£	

(d) The cost of the Volvo in the taxable benefit computation is:

£	

(e) The taxable benefit in respect of the provision of the Volvo for private use in 2016/17 is:

£	

(f) The taxable benefit in respect of the provision of fuel for the Volvo for private use in 2016/17 is:

£	

Task 2

(a) Elizabeth's employer provided her with a television for her private use on 6 April 2016, costing £2,500. Elizabeth did not pay anything for the use of the TV.

(1) The taxable benefit for 2016/17 is:

£	

Elizabeth buys the TV from her employer for £750 on 5 April 2017, when it is worth £1,875.

(2) The taxable benefit for 2016/17 is:

£	

(b) Indicate whether the following benefits would be taxable or exempt if provided in 2016/17, by ticking the boxes:

Item	Taxable	Exempt
Provision of second mobile phone		
Removal costs of £7,500		
Provision of parking space at work		
Accommodation provided to a caretaker for proper performance of his employment duties		
Membership of fitness club		

Task 3

(a) Millie is employed by RST plc. For each of the following payments, state the amount of employment income taxable in 2016/17. If an amount is not taxable in 2016/17 enter 0.

(1) Monthly salary of £2,000. Millie becomes entitled to each month's salary on the 25th of each month and it is paid to her on the 28th of each month. Due to a bank error, the salary for March 2016 was not paid to her until 10 April 2016.

The employment income for 2016/17 is:

£	

(2) Commission of £1,200 paid with her April 2017 salary. The commission relates to sales made in the month of March 2017.

The employment income for 2016/17 is:

£	

(3) Bonus of £5,000 paid on 30 April 2016 based on company's accounting profit for the year ended 31 December 2015.

The employment income for 2016/17 is:

£	

(4) Reimbursement of business expenses of £500 in December 2016.

The employment income for 2016/17 is:

£	

(b) In 2016/17, Calum had the following income:

Salary	£47,900
Building society interest	£180
Dividends	£100

Calum made a contribution of £2,500 to his employer's occupational pension scheme.

Using the proforma layout provided, prepare a computation of taxable income for 2016/17, clearly showing the distinction between the different types of income. Both brackets and minus signs can be used to show negative numbers.

	Non-savings income £	Savings income £	Dividend income £	Total £

Task 4

(a) Jim, an additional rate taxpayer, received £10,000 of bank interest and £5,500 of dividends during 2016/17. Of these amounts, £500 of interest and £300 of dividends were from his ISA accounts.

(1) Calculate the amount of interest on which Jim will pay income tax at a rate greater than 0% in 2016/17.

£	

(2) Calculate the amount of dividends on which Jim will pay income tax at a rate greater than 0% in 2016/17.

£	

(b) Myrtle has the following income for 2016/17: pension income of £105,000, bank interest of £4,800 and dividends of £3,600. She made net contributions of £2,400 to her personal pension scheme during 2016/17.

(1) Myrtle's adjusted net income for 2016/17 is:

£	

(2) Myrtle's taxable income (before the savings and dividend allowances) for 2016/17 is:

£	

Task 5

(a) Is the following statement true or false?

Property income for a tax year is calculated by taking rental income accrued in the tax year less expenses paid in the tax year.

	✓
True	
False	

(b) Zhu Liu bought an apartment on 1 October 2016. He let it out, unfurnished, from 1 December 2016 at an annual rent of £18,000 payable quarterly in advance. He incurred the following expenses in relation to the property:

	£
General repairs and maintenance, all incurred prior to 5 April 2017	750
Insurance for the 12 month period ended 30 September 2017	300
Decorating paid for on 31 March 2017, for work carried out on 10 April 2017	500
Installing a shower	1,500

Using the proforma layout provided, calculate the property income for 2016/17. Fill in all the unshaded boxes. If an expense is not allowable, enter 0. Both brackets and minus signs can be used to show negative numbers.

	£
Rental income	
Repairs	
Insurance	
Decorating	
Shower	
Property income	

Task 6

(a) Ian has had the following amounts of taxable income (AFTER deduction of his personal allowance) for 2016/17:

	£
Non-savings income	38,382
Savings income	680
Dividend income	5,400

Ian paid £100 to Oxfam in November 2016 and made a Gift Aid declaration.

Ian's tax liability on each source of income for 2016/17 is as follows:

(1) Non-savings income:

£	

(2) Savings income:

£	

(3) Dividend income:

£	

(b) **(1)** Max earns £2,500 in 2016/17 in a part-time job. He also has property income of £15,000 in 2016/17 from letting out a field.

The maximum personal pension contribution on which Max can get tax relief in 2016/17 is:

	✓
£2,500	
£3,600	
£17,500	
£5,000	

(2) **Max's tax liability for 2016/17 is:**

£	

Task 7

(a) A client has told you that she forgot to include some bank interest in the tax return you prepared and she does not intend to tell HMRC of the omission.

What TWO actions should you take?

	✓
Inform the Association of Accounting Technicians about the omission	
Report the client's refusal and the facts surrounding it to your firm's Money Laundering Reporting Officer	
Inform the client in writing that it is not possible for you to act for her in connection with that return	
Inform HMRC about the omission	

(b) Mike is wishing to sell several assets in 2016/17 and the gains will be more than his annual exemption. He has £3,000 left of his basic rate band. His civil partner, Rob, will not be using his annual exemption this year and is a basic rate taxpayer.

What advice would you give your client in order to minimise his tax liability on the sale of the assets.

Task 8

(a) Which TWO of the following statements are true about inheritance tax?

(1) It is an indirect tax.
(2) It is a progressive tax.
(3) It is an environmental tax.
(4) It is a direct tax.

	✓
1 and 3	
1 and 4	
2 and 3	
2 and 4	

(b) Which TWO of the following statements concerning tax evasion and tax avoidance are correct?

	✓
Tax evasion is illegal	
Both tax evasion and tax avoidance are illegal	
Tax avoidance involves any legal method of reducing the taxpayer's tax burden	
Tax evasion always involves providing HM Revenue & Customs with false information	

(c) Which TWO of the following statements are correct about how your firm should deal with the suggestion from a client that no disclosure is made to HMRC of their capital gain?

	✓
The client should be advised to disclose details of the capital gain to HMRC	
If the client does not disclose the gain to HMRC, your firm can definitely still continue to act for him	
If your firm ceases to act for to client, it must disclose this to HMRC and provide detailed reasons why it has ceased to act	
If the client does not disclose the gain to HMRC, your firm would be obliged to report under the money laundering regulations.	

Task 9

(a) Classify whether a disposal of each of the following assets will be chargeable to or exempt from capital gains tax:

Asset	Chargeable	Exempt
Plot of land sold for £20,000		
Diamond brooch sold for £3,500 which cost £2,000		
Shares in an unlisted company sold for £10,000		
1930 Rolls Royce car sold for £100,000		

(b) Jaycee made the following gains and loss in 2016/17:

	£
Gain on shares September 2016	18,500
Gain on painting December 2016	6,000
Gain on statue January 2017	18,895
Loss on vase April 2016	(10,000)

Jaycee is a higher rate taxpayer.

(1) Her capital gains tax liability for 2016/17 is:

£	

(2) The due date for payment of this liability is: (enter date as xx/xx/xxxx)

(c) In December 2016, Mabel gave her son an asset worth £20,000. She had acquired the asset for £25,000.

In March 2017, Mabel gave her sister an asset worth £30,000. Mabel had acquired the asset for £22,000.

Mabel's chargeable gains (before the annual exempt amount) for 2016/17 are:

£	

Task 10

Ming Lee bought 1,000 shares in Lavender Ltd for £5,000 in October 2005. In May 2007, she received 200 shares in a bonus issue. In January 2011 the company offered a rights issue at 1 share for every 6 held. She accepted this rights issue at £3 per share. She sold 1,000 shares in Lavender Ltd in January 2017 for £12,400.

Clearly showing the balance of shares and their value to carry forward, calculate the chargeable gain on sale of the shares. All workings must be shown.

Task 11

(a) On 1 March 1996, Craig bought a house for £36,000. He had lived in it until 1 September 1999, when he went to Australia to take up employment. He returned from there on 1 September 2005 and moved back into the house until 1 February 2011 when he purchased a small flat. He has lived in the flat since then. Craig finally sold the house for £178,000 on 31 October 2016.

Using the proforma layout below, show the chargeable gain on sale. Both brackets and minus signs can be used to show negative numbers.

Chargeable gain on sale of property	£
Proceeds of sale	
Less allowable cost	
Gain before PPR	
Less PPR exempt amount	
Chargeable gain	

(b) During 2016/17 Nina has sold an asset giving rise to a chargeable gain of £20,100. She has capital losses brought forward at 6 April 2016 of £11,000.

The amount of capital losses Nina will have to carry forward at 5 April 2017 is:

	✓
£2,000	
£0	
£11,000	
£9,000	

Task 12

Ada died on 25 April 2016. Her death estate was valued at £623,000. Her executors paid funeral expenses of £3,000 on 12 May 2016. Under the terms of her will Ada left £150,000 to her husband, a specific legacy of £40,000 to her sister, and the residue of the estate to her children. She has no nil band available on death.

How much inheritance tax would be due on her death estate?

	✓
£172,000	
£58,000	
£248,000	
£188,000	

Task 13

Afiya died on 29 November 2016. She had made the following gifts during her lifetime:

(1) On 14 September 2014, Afiya made a gift of 6,500 £1 ordinary shares in Cassava Ltd, an unquoted investment company, to her daughter.

Before the transfer Afiya owned 8,000 shares out of Cassava Ltd's issued share capital of 10,000 £1 ordinary shares. On 14 September 2014, Cassava Ltd's shares were worth £3 each for a holding of 15%, £7 each for a holding of 65%, and £8 each for a holding of 80%.

(2) On 27 January 2015, Afiya made a cash gift of £400,000 to a trust. Afiya paid the inheritance tax arising from this gift.

Calculate the lifetime tax paid, and the death tax arising on these gifts as a result of her death.

This style of question would be human marked in the exam.

BPP PRACTICE ASSESSMENT 4
PERSONAL TAX

ANSWERS

Personal Tax (PLTX)
BPP practice assessment 4

Task 1

(a) The cost of the Ford Focus in the taxable benefit computation is:

£	21,000

(b) The taxable benefit in respect of the provision of the Ford Focus for private use in 2016/17 is:

£	2,363

£21,000 × 15% (CO_2 emissions of 90g/km) × 9/12

(c) The taxable benefit in respect of the provision of fuel for the Ford Focus for private use in 2016/17 is:

£	2,498

£22,200 × 15% × 9/12 (no reduction for partial reimbursement of private fuel)

(d) The cost of the Volvo in the taxable benefit computation is:

£	22,000

£27,000 – £5,000 (max deduction for capital contribution)

(e) The taxable benefit in respect of the provision of the Volvo for private use in 2016/17 is:

£	1,870

£22,000 × 34% × 3/12
170 – 95 = 75
75 ÷ 5 = 15%
16% + 15% + 3% (diesel) = 34%

(f) The taxable benefit in respect of the provision of fuel for the Volvo for private use in 2016/17 is:

£	1,887

£22,200 × 34% × 3/12 (no reduction for partial reimbursement of private fuel)

Task 2

(a) **(1)** The taxable benefit for 2016/17 is:

£	500

Use of asset £2,500 × 20%

(2) The taxable benefit for 2016/17 is:

£	1,250

Greater of:

	£
(i) Original market value	2,500
Less assessed for use 2016/17	(500)
	2,000
(ii) Market value at acquisition by employee	1,875

Greater = £2,000 less amount paid by Elizabeth of £750

(b)

Item	Taxable	Exempt
Provision of second mobile phone	✓	
Removal costs of £7,500		✓
Provision of parking space at work		✓
Accommodation provided to a caretaker for proper performance of his employment duties		✓
Membership of fitness club	✓	

Task 3

(a) **(1)** The employment income for 2016/17 is:

£	24,000

April 2016 to March 2017 = 12 × £2,000

The salary for March 2016 was received for tax purposes on 25 March 2016 when Millie became entitled to it and so was taxed in 2015/16.

(2) The employment income for 2016/17 is:

£	0

Commission received 25 April 2017 (taxed in 2017/18)

(3) The employment income for 2016/17 is:

£	5,000

Bonus received 30 April 2016

(4) The employment income for 2016/17 is:

£	0

This is exempt as the reimbursement is covered by an allowable deduction.

(b)

	Non-savings income £	Savings income £	Dividend income £	Total £
Employment income:				
Salary	47,900			
Less occupational pension contribution	(2,500)			
Employment income	45,400			
Building society interest		180		
Dividends			100	
Net income	45,400	180	100	45,680
Less personal allowance	(11,000)			(11,000)
Taxable income	34,400	180	100	34,680

Task 4

(a) **(1)** The amount of interest on which Jim will pay income tax at a rate greater than 0% in 2016/17 is:

£	9,500

ISA interest is exempt. No savings allowance due

(2) The amount of dividends on which Jim will pay income tax at a rate greater than 0% in 2016/17 is:

£	200

£5,500 – £5,000 dividend allowance – £300 ISA dividends (exempt)

(b) **(1)** Myrtle's adjusted net income for 2016/17 is:

£	110,400

	Total £
Pension income	105,000
Bank interest	4,800
Dividends	3,600
Total income	113,400
Less: pension contributions (£2,400 × 100/80)	(3,000)
Adjusted net income	110,400

(2) Myrtle's taxable income (before the savings and dividend allowances) for 2016/17 is:

£	107,600

	£
Adjusted net income	110,400
Less income limit	(100,000)
Excess	10,400
Personal allowance	11,000
Less half excess	(5,200)
	5,800

Taxable income is therefore: £113,400 – £5,800 = £107,600

Task 5

(a)

	✓
True	
False	✓

Property income for a tax year is calculated by taking rental income accrued in the tax year less expenses accrued in the tax year.

(b)

	£
Rental income £18,000 × 4/12	6,000
Repairs	(750)
Insurance £300 × 6/12	(150)
Decorating (not accrued in 2016/17)	0
Shower (capital expense)	0
Property income	5,100

Task 6

(a) **(1)** Non-savings income:

£	8,928

	£
£32,000 × 20%	6,400
£125 (£100 × 100/80) × 20% (extended band)	25
£6,257 × 40% (£38,382 – £32,000 – £125)	2,503
	8,928

(2) Savings income:

£	72

£500 × 0% + £180 × 40%

(3) Dividend income:

£	130

£5,000 × 0% + £400 × 32.5%

(b) **(1)** The maximum personal pension contribution on which Max can get tax relief in 2016/17 is:

	✓
£2,500	
£3,600	✓
£17,500	
£5,000	

Higher of earnings and £3,600. Property income is not relevant earnings unless from a qualifying holiday accommodation.

(2) Max's tax liability for 2016/17 is:

£	1,300

Total income is £2,500 + £15,000 = £17,500, less PA of £11,000 = £6,500

Income tax is £6,500 × 20% = £1,300

As he is a basic rate taxpayer he will obtain full relief at source on any pension payments he makes so there is no need to factor them into the calculation.

Task 7

(a)

	✓
Inform the Association of Accounting Technicians about the omission	
Report the client's refusal and the facts surrounding it to your firm's Money Laundering Reporting Officer	✓
Inform the client in writing that it is not possible for you to act for her in connection with that return	✓
Inform HMRC about the omission	

(b)

Transfers between civil partners are at no gain no loss and so Mike could transfer assets to Rob sufficient to make gains up to Rob's annual exemption.

If Mike is then left with gains of more than £14,100 (his annual exemption of £11,100 plus his unused basic rate band of £3,000) then he will have to consider transferring more to Rob so that the gains are taxed at the basic rate of 10% rather than the higher rate of 20%.

The issue with this is that the transfers have to be 'no strings attached' so Mike could not ask Rob for the net proceeds of these sales once all the transactions have taken place and the tax has been paid. This is something that Mike and Rob will have to discuss between them.

An alternative would be for Mike to delay the sale of some of the assets so that he has two annual exemptions available (2016/17 and 2017/18). This would enable Mike to retain the sale proceeds from those assets.

Task 8

(a)

	✓
1 and 3	
1 and 4	
2 and 3	
2 and 4	✓

Inheritance tax is a progressive tax as the proportion of the wealth that is taxable increases as wealth increases (the amount covered by the nil rate band is charged at 0% and the remainder at 20% (in life) or 40% (on death)).

Inheritance tax is a direct tax as it is on a specific individual's wealth.

(b)

	✓
Tax evasion is illegal	✓
Both tax evasion and tax avoidance are illegal	
Tax avoidance involves any legal method of reducing the taxpayer's tax burden	✓
Tax evasion always involves providing HM Revenue & Customs with false information	

Tax evasion is illegal and Tax avoidance involves any legal method of reducing the taxpayer's tax burden.

Tax evasion does not necessarily involve providing HM Revenue & Customs (HMRC) with false information. It could include this situation where a taxpayer is evading tax by not providing HMRC with information to which it is entitled.

(c)

	✓
The client should be advised to disclose details of the capital gain to HMRC	✓
If the client does not disclose the gain to HMRC, your firm can definitely still continue to act for him	
If your firm ceases to act for to client, it must disclose this to HMRC and provide detailed reasons why it has ceased to act	
If the client does not disclose the gain to HMRC, your firm would be obliged to report under the money laundering regulations.	✓

The client should be advised to disclose details of the capital gain to HMRC and if the client does not disclose the gain to HMRC, your firm would be obliged to report under the money laundering regulations.

Your firm should also consider ceasing to act for the client. If it does cease to act, your firm should notify HMRC that it no longer acts for him although your firm should not provide any reason for this.

Task 9

(a)

Asset	Chargeable	Exempt
Plot of land sold for £20,000	✓	
Diamond brooch sold for £3,500 which cost £2,000		✓ (Chattel – cost and proceeds no more than £6,000)
Shares in an unlisted company sold for £10,000	✓	
1930 Rolls Royce car sold for £100,000		✓ (all cars exempt)

(b) **(1)** Her capital gains tax liability for 2016/17 is:

£	4,459

	£
Gain on shares	18,500
Gain on painting	6,000
Gain on statue	18,895
Chargeable gains	43,395
Less allowable loss on vase	(10,000)
Net chargeable gains for year	33,395
Less annual exempt amount	(11,100)
Taxable gains	22,295
CGT: £22,295 × 20% (higher rate taxpayer)	4,459

(2) The due date for payment of this liability is:

31/01/2018

(c) Mabel's chargeable gains (before the annual exempt amount) for 2016/17 are:

£	8,000

	£
Gift to her sister:	
Deemed proceeds of sale (market value)	30,000
Less allowable cost	(22,000)
Chargeable gain	8,000

Both the son and the sister are connected persons for Mabel. However, the loss of £5,000 on the disposal to the son can only be set against gains made to him, not to another connected person.

Task 10

Share pool

	No of shares	**Cost £**
October 2005 Acquisition	1,000	5,000
May 2007 Bonus	200	Nil
	1,200	5,000
January 2011 Rights 1 for 6 × £3 (1/6 × 1,200 = 200 shares × £3 = £600)	200	600
	1,400	5,600
January 2017 Disposal (1,000/1,400 × £5,600)	(1,000)	(4,000)
c/f	400	1,600
Gain		
Proceeds of sale		12,400
Less allowable cost		(4,000)
Chargeable gain		8,400

Task 11

(a)

Chargeable gain on sale of property	£
Proceeds of sale	178,000
Less allowable cost	(36,000)
Gain before PPR	142,000
Less PPR exempt amount	(112,798)
Chargeable gain	29,202

Working:

Time period	Chargeable months	Exempt months	Total months
1.3.96 to 31.8.99		42	42
1.9.99 to 31.8.05 (Note 1)		72	72
1.9.05 to 31.1.11		65	65
1.2.11 to 31.10.16 (Note 2)	51	18	69
	51	197	248

Notes

1. Any period of employment abroad is treated as deemed occupation if it is preceded and followed by actual occupation.
2. Last 18 months of ownership is always exempt if the property has been the taxpayer's only or main residence at some time during the ownership period.

(b) The amount of capital losses Nina will have to carry forward at 5 April 2017 is:

	✓
£2,000	✓
£0	
£11,000	
£9,000	

The capital loss brought forward will be used to bring the chargeable gain for 2016/17 to the level of the annual exempt amount. This uses £9,000 of the loss leaving £2,000 to carry forward to 2017/18.

Task 12

	✓
£172,000	
£58,000	
£248,000	
£188,000	✓

Death estate

	£
Assets at death	623,000
Less funeral expenses	(3,000)
Value of estate for IHT purposes	620,000
Less exempt legacy to spouse	(150,000)
Chargeable estate	470,000
IHT liability £470,000 × 40%	188,000

Task 13

Lifetime transfers

14 September 2014:

	£
Value of shares held before transfer 8,000 × £8	64,000
Less value of shares held after transfer 1,500 × £3	(4,500)
Transfer of value	59,500
Less: annual exemption 2014/15	(3,000)
annual exemption 2013/14 b/f	(3,000)
Potentially exempt transfer	53,500

27 January 2015:

	£
Net chargeable transfer	400,000
IHT	
325,000 × 0%	0
75,000 × 20/80 (donor pays tax)	18,750
400,000	18,750
Gross chargeable transfer £(400,000 + 18,750)	418,750

Additional tax on lifetime transfer on death of donor

14 September 2014:

Potentially exempt transfer of £53,500 becomes chargeable as donor dies within seven years.

Within nil rate band at death, no tax to pay.

27 January 2015:

Nil rate band available £(325,000 – 53,500) = £271,500.

	£
Gross chargeable transfer	418,750
IHT	
271,500 × 0%	0
147,250 × 40%	58,900
418,750	58,900
No taper relief (death within three years of transfer)	
Less lifetime tax paid	(18,750)
Additional tax payable on death	40,150

BPP PRACTICE ASSESSMENT 5 PERSONAL TAX

Time allowed: 2.5 hours

PRACTICE ASSESSMENT 5

BPP LEARNING MEDIA

Personal Tax (PLTX)
BPP practice assessment 5

Task 1

(a) Yan is provided with a company car for business and private use throughout 2016/17. The car had a list price of £17,200 when bought new in December 2015, although the company paid £16,000 for the car after a dealer discount. Yan made a contribution of £2,000 to the cost of the car.

The car has a petrol engine and has CO_2 emissions of 107g/km. The company pays for all running costs, including all fuel. Yan does not make any contribution for his private use of the car.

(1) The cost of the car in the taxable benefit computation is:

£	

(2) The percentage used in the taxable benefit computation is:

	%

(3) The taxable benefit in respect of the provision offuel for private use is:

£	

(b) You have received the following email from Matt Taylor:

From: MTaylor@boxmail.net
To: AATStudent@boxmail.net
Sent: 14 June 2017 11:35
Subject: Car

I have recently been promoted and now have to do some travelling by car on business, probably about 6,000 miles a year. My employer has given me two options:

(1) A company car with a list price of £15,000. It has a petrol engine. The car is environmentally friendly and so has CO_2 emissions of only 85g/km. I will be able to use the car for both business and private purposes, but I will be required to repay the cost of my private fuel.

(2) A mileage allowance of 35p per business mile if I use my own car.

Can you please explain the taxation aspects of each of the options?

Thanks, Matt

Reply to Matt's email

From:	AATStudent@boxmail.net
To:	MTaylor@boxmail.net
Sent:	16 June 2017 10:41
Subject:	Car

Task 2

(a) (1) Marge has recently started to work for LMN plc and earns £30,000 a year. She is entitled to childcare vouchers of £60 per week for 45 weeks in 2016/17.

The taxable benefit for 2016/17 is:

£	

(2) **Tick to show if the following statement is true or false.**

The maximum amount of exempt benefit for the additional costs of home working is £4 per week.

	✓
True	
False	

(b) For each of the following benefits, tick whether they would be wholly or partly taxable or wholly exempt if received in 2016/17:

Item	Wholly or partly taxable	Wholly exempt
Award of £25 under staff suggestion scheme		
Removal expenses of £9,000		
Incidental personal expenses of working away from home in the UK of £10 per night		
Staff party at cost of £100 per head		

(c) Antonia is employed by Zed Ltd. She receives store vouchers from the company as a Christmas bonus in December 2016. These enable her to buy goods worth £300. Her employer bought the vouchers from the store for £267.

(1) The taxable benefit for 2016/17 is:

£	

Antonia is also loaned £12,000 by Zed Ltd on 1 July 2016. She pays interest at an annual rate of 0.5% on the loan. She does not make any capital repayments in 2016/17.

(2) The taxable benefit for 2016/17 is:

£	

Task 3

Andrea is a director of Z Ltd and provides you with the following information:

(1) Monthly salary of £7,500 paid on 25th day of each month.

(2) Bonus A of £17,500 based on company's accounting profit for the period of account ended 31 March 2016, determined on 31 October 2016. Andrea became entitled to be paid this bonus on 30 April 2017 and it was actually paid to her on 30 June 2017.

(3) Bonus B of £22,500 based on the company's accounting profit for the period of account ended 31 July 2017, determined on 31 March 2017. Andrea became entitled to be paid this bonus on 30 June 2017 and it was actually paid to her on 30 September 2017.

(4) 5% of basic salary paid into the company pension scheme each tax year, Z Ltd matches these contributions.

(5) Use of a company car which has a taxable benefit for 2016/17 of £3,250. No fuel is provided for private use.

(6) Dividends received of £4,222, and interest of £750 from an ISA.

Complete the following table showing the figures to be included in Andrea's taxable income for 2016/17. Use whole pounds only. If your answer is zero, please insert a '0'. Do not use brackets or minus signs.

	£
Salary	
Bonus A	
Bonus B	
Director's pension contribution	
Company's pension contribution	
Company car benefit	
Dividends	
Interest from ISA	
Net income	
Personal allowance	
Taxable income	

Task 4

(a) During 2016/17, Mimi received the following income. In each case, show the amount of income that she should enter on her tax return. If the income is exempt, enter 0.

(1) Property income £2,000.

£	

(2) Premium bond prize £100.

£	

(3) Government stock interest £80.

£	

(4) Dividends received from an ISA of £2,000.

£	

(b) Marcello receives a dividend of £5,400 in March 2016. He is an additional rate taxpayer.

(1) The amount of the dividend that Marcello will pay income tax on at a rate greater than 0% is:

£	

(2) The tax payable on the dividend is:

£	

(3) Marcello also has some building society interest.

Is the following statement true or false?

Marcello will pay tax at 0% on the first £500 of this interest.

	✓
True	
False	

Task 5

(a) Ronnie buys a house on 6 May 2016 and rents it out on 6 August 2016. He charges an annual rent of £9,000, payable in advance. He pays an annual insurance premium on 6 June 2016 of £600.

Ronnie's taxable property income for 2016/17 is:

£	

(b) A client, Mohamed Albayouk, has sent in the following information for 2016/17 in relation to his two properties that he rents out.

17 Wool Lane is unfurnished and is rented out at £560 per month. 42 Silk Street is furnished and is rented out at £800 per month. Both properties were occupied throughout 2016/17.

The expenses for the year were:

Item	17 Wool Lane £	42 Silk Street £
Insurance	300	280
Water rates	160	176
Council tax	1,800	2,100
Cleaning	800	500
Redecoration	1,000	0
Cost of replacement furniture	0	3,450

Calculate the property income taxable on MohamedAlbayouk for 2016/17 using the proforma layout provided. Fill in all the unshaded boxes. If any item is not an allowable expense, enter 0. Both brackets and minus signs can be used to show negative numbers.

	17 Wool Lane £	42 Silk Street £
Income:		
Rents		
Expenses:		
Insurance		
Water rates		
Council tax		
Cleaning		
Redecoration		
Replacement furniture relief		
Property income		
Total property income		

(c) Asif owns three properties which he lets out throughout 2016/17. He makes a profit of £5,000 on Property 1, a loss of £1,200 on Property 2 and a profit of £2,000 on Property 3. Asif also has a property loss of £1,500 brought forward at 5 April 2016.

The property income taxable on Asif for 2016/17 is:

£	

Task 6

Andrew, born in 1966, has income as follows:

	£
Employment income	46,000
Bank interest received	1,600
Dividends received	9,500

Andrew makes a Gift Aid donation of £1,200 in July 2016.

(a) Calculate his total income tax liability for 2016/17, using the table given below. Both brackets and minus signs can be used to show negative numbers.

	£

(b) On which dates are payment on accounts due for 2016/17?

	✓
31 January 2017 and 31 July 2017	
31 January 2018 and 31 July 2018	
31 July 2017 and 31 January 2018	
31 October 2017 and 31 January 2018	

Task 7

(a) Which of the following taxpayers is UK resident for the tax year 2016/17 on the basis of the information given?

(1) Suzy, previously UK resident, present in UK between 6 April 2016 and 5 December 2017

(2) Miles, not previously UK resident, present in UK between 6 April 2016 and 5 May 2016

	✓
1 and 2	
1 only	
2 only	
Neither 1 nor 2	

(b) Which TWO of the following types of income are exempt from income tax?

(1) Interest on an NS&I Investment account
(2) Premium bond prizes
(3) Interest on UK Government stocks ('gilts')
(4) Dividends on shares held in an Individual Savings Account

	✓
1 and 2	
1 and 4	
2 and 3	
2 and 4	

(c) Sarah has a salary of £46,000. She also has the use of a company car with a taxable benefit if £3,850.

What national insurance contributions are suffered by her employer? Give your answer to the nearest £1.

Class 1 Primary

£	

Class 1 Secondary

£	

Class 1A

£	

Task 8

(a) You are a sole practitioner and suspect that one of your clients may be engaged in money laundering.

Who should you inform about your suspicions?

	✓
National Crime Agency	
Association of Taxation Technicians	
Tax Tribunal	
HM Treasury	

(b) On 30 September 2017 your client, Jakki, leaves the following message on your voicemail:

'Hi, it's Jakki. I know that I am a new client to your practice and that you did not prepare my tax return for 2015/16, but I have just discovered that I failed to notify HMRC of some dividends that I received in January 2016. I simply forgot about them, but I am worried that HMRC will find out that I have not paid the right amount of tax on this income. Can you please advise about what I should do? Thanks.'

List the information that you need to give Jakki when you ring her back to discuss this issue.

Task 9

(a) For each of the following assets, tick whether they are chargeable or exempt assets for capital gains tax:

Asset	Chargeable	Exempt
Horse		
Field in which horse is kept		
Antique horse brass costing £500, worth £1,700		

(b) Ulma bought a holiday cottage for £65,000 and spent £15,000 on an extension and £10,000 on redecoration. She sold the cottage for £125,000 on 10 August 2016.

The chargeable gain on sale is:

£	

(c) Jade purchased an emerald bracelet for £8,000. She sold the bracelet in August 2016 at auction for £2,700 (which was net of 10% commission).

The allowable loss on sale is:

£	

Task 10

Merrill paid £5,000 for 2,000 shares in Bug plc in August 2009. In September 2012, there was a one for one bonus issue. Merrill sold 1,000 shares in June 2016 for £8,000.

Compute the chargeable gain and the value of the share pool following the disposal, using the proforma layout provided. Both brackets and minus signs can be used to show negative numbers.

Gain

	£

Share pool

	No of shares	Cost £

Task 11

(a) Jai makes chargeable gains (on antiques) of £15,100 in November 2016. Jai's taxable income for 2016/17 is £31,390 and he made a Gift Aid payment of £400 to Oxfam in May 2016.

The CGT payable for 2016/17 is:

£	

(b) **Tick to show if the following statement is true or false.**

The last 18 months of ownership of a house are exempt provided that the house is lived in by the owner at some time during that 18-month period.

	✓
True	
False	

Task 12

(a) On 7 July 2010, Paul made a gross chargeable transfer (after all exemptions) of £260,000. On 19 December 2016 he gave £190,000 to a trust. Paul agreed to pay any lifetime IHT due.

How much inheritance tax will be payable by Paul on the December 2016 transfer of value?

	✓
£28,250	
£31,250	
£29,750	
£23,800	

(b) Dan owned all 1,000 shares in Z Ltd, an unquoted investment company. On 10 October 2016, Dan gave 300 of his shares in Z Ltd to his daughter. The values of the shares on 10 October 2016 were as follows:

% shareholding	Value per share £
76 – 100	150
51 – 75	120
26 – 50	90
1 – 25	30

What is the diminution in value of Dan's estate as a result of his gift on 10 October 2016?

	✓
£123,000	
£27,000	
£66,000	
£18,000	

(c) Susanna died on 19 November 2016. Her estate consisted of a house worth £200,000 (on which there was a repayment mortgage of £60,000) and investments and cash totalling £350,000. Her executors paid funeral expenses of £5,000. Susanna left a cash legacy of £100,000 to her husband and the residue of her estate to her son and daughter. Susanna had not made any lifetime transfers of value.

How much inheritance tax will be payable on Susanna's estate?

£	

Task 13

Kendra died in January 2017, aged 93. She has made no lifetime gifts and owned the following assets at death.

Kendra owns the following assets:

(1) A property valued at £970,000.

(2) Building society deposits of £387,000.

(3) Investments in Individual Savings Accounts (ISAs) valued at £39,000 and savings certificates from NS&I (National Savings and Investments) valued at £17,000.

(4) A life assurance policy on her own life. Proceeds of £225,000 will be received following Kendra's death.

The cost of Kendra's funeral will be £12,800. She also has an outstanding unsecured loan of £1,200 which is due to be repaid on her death.

Under the terms of her will, Kendra has left her entire estate to her children.

The nil rate band of Kendra's husband was fully utilised when he died ten years ago.

Calculate the IHT due on Kendra's death.

(This style of question would be human marked in the exam)

BPP PRACTICE ASSESSMENT 5 PERSONAL TAX

ANSWERS

Personal Tax (PLTX)
BPP practice assessment 5

Task 1

(a) **(1)** The cost of the car in the taxable benefit computation is:

£	15,200

List price less capital contribution made by Yan.

(2) The percentage used in the taxable benefit computation is:

18	%

105 – 95 = 10
10 ÷ 5 = 2%
16% + 2%

(3) The taxable benefit in respect of the provision offuel for private use is:

£	3,996

£22,200 × 18%

(b)

From: AATStudent@boxmail.net
To: MTaylor@boxmail.net
Sent: 16 June 2017 10:41
Subject: Car

The provision of the company car will be a taxable benefit because it is available for private use. The benefit is the list price of the car multiplied by a percentage. In this case, because the car has CO_2 emissions of between 76g/km and 94g/km, the percentage will be 15%. The benefit will therefore be £15,000 × 15% = £2,250 per tax year. There will be no fuel benefit because you will be reimbursing the cost of your private fuel.

There is a statutory mileage allowance which would apply if you use your own car for business purposes. The rate is 45p per mile up to 10,000 miles per year. As your employer would only be paying you 35p per mile, the extra 10p per mile could be claimed by you as an allowable deduction when working out your employment income. If you travelled 6,000 business miles in a tax year, the deduction would be 6,000 × 10p = £600.

Task 2

(a) **(1)** The taxable benefit for 2016/17 is:

£	225

£(60 – 55) = £5 × 45

(2)

	✓
True	
False	✓

Payments in excess of £4 per week can be exempt benefits provided that evidence will be given that the payment is wholly in respect of additional household expenses incurred by the employee in carrying out his duties at home.

(b)

Item	Wholly or partly taxable	Wholly exempt
Award of £25 under staff suggestion scheme		✓
Removal expenses of £9,000	✓ (limit £8,000)	
Incidental personal expenses of working away from home in the UK of £10 per night	✓ (wholly taxable if exceeds £5)	
Staff party at cost of £100 per head		✓(up to £150)

(c) **(1)** The taxable benefit for 2016/17 is:

£	267

Non-cash voucher therefore cost to employer.

If it was a cash voucher the benefit would be face value.

(2) The taxable benefit for 2016/17 is:

£	225

£12,000 × (3 – 0.5)% × 9/12

Task 3

	£
Salary (£7,500 × 12)	90,000
Bonus A (treated as received on 31 October 2016)	17,500
Bonus B (treated as received on 30 June 2017 – taxed in 2017/18)	0
Director's pension contribution (£90,000 × 5%)	(4,500)
Company's pension contribution (exempt benefit)	0
Company car benefit	3,250
Dividends	4,222
Interest from ISA	0
Net income	110,472
Personal allowance £(11,000 – ((110,472 – 100,000)/2))	5,764
Taxable income	104,708

Task 4

(a) **(1)** Property income £2,000.

£	2,000

(2) Premium bond prize £100.

£	0

Exempt

(3) Government stock interest £80.

£	80

(4) Dividends received from an ISA of £2,000.

£	0

ISA income is exempt

(b) **(1)** The amount of the dividend that Marcello will pay income tax on at a rate greater than 0% is:

£	400

£5,400 – £5,000 dividend allowance

(2) The tax payable on the dividend is:

£	152

£400 × 38.1%

(3)

	✓
True	
False	✓

Additional rate taxpayers do not receive a savings allowance.

Task 5

(a) Ronnie's taxable property income for 2016/17 is:

£	5,500

	£
Rent accrued £9,000 × 8/12	6,000
Less expense £600 × 10/12	(500)
Property income 2016/17	5,500

Income and expenses are taxed on the accruals basis.

(b)

	17 Wool Lane £	42 Silk Street £
Income:		
Rents£560/800 × 12	6,720	9,600
Expenses:		
Insurance	(300)	(280)
Water rates	(160)	(176)
Council tax	(1,800)	(2,100)
Cleaning	(800)	(500)
Redecoration	(1,000)	0
Replacement furniture relief	0	(3,450)
Property income	2,660	3,094
Total property income	5,754	

(c) The property income taxable on Asif for 2016/17 is:

£	4,300

	£
Property 1 profit	5,000
Property 2 loss	(1,200)
Property 3 profit	2,000
	5,800
Less loss b/f	(1,500)
Property income 2016/17	4,300

Task 6

(a)

	£
Employment income	46,000
Bank interest	1,600
Dividends	9,500
	57,100
Personal allowance	(11,000)
Taxable income	46,100
Tax on non-savings income:	
£32,000 × 20%	6,400
£1,500 (£1,200 × 100/80) × 20%	300
£1,500 × 40% (£46,000 – £11,000) £35,000 – £32,000 – £1,500)	600
Tax on savings income:	
£500 × 0% + £1,100 × 40%	440

	£
Tax on dividend income:	
£5,000 × 0% + £4,500 × 32½ %	1,463
Income Tax Liability	9,203

(b) On which dates are payment on accounts due for 2016/17?

	✓
31 January 2017 and 31 July 2017	✓
31 January 2018 and 31 July 2018	
31 July 2017 and 31 January 2018	
31 October 2017 and 31 January 2018	

Payments on account are due on 31 January in the tax year and 31 July following the end of the tax year.

Task 7

(a)

	✓
1 and 2	
1 only	✓
2 only	
Neither 1 nor 2	

Suzy is UK resident in the tax year 2016/17 as she is present in the UK for 183 days or more (meets automatic UK test).

Miles is not UK resident in the tax year 2016/17 as he was not previously UK resident and is present in the UK for less than 46 days (meets automatic overseas test).

(b)

	✓
1 and 2	
1 and 4	
2 and 3	
2 and 4	✓

Interest on an NS&I Investment account and interest on UK Government stocks ('gilts') are taxable.

Premium bond prizes and dividends on shares held in an Individual Savings Account are exempt.

(c) **Class 1 Primary**

£	0

Note. Class 1 primary is suffered by the employee.

Class 1 Secondary

£	5,229

Workings: £(46,000 – 8,112) × 13.8%

Class 1A

£	531

Workings: £3,850 × 13.8%

Task 8

(a)

	✓
National Crime Agency	✓
Association of Taxation Technicians	
Tax Tribunal	
HM Treasury	

(b)

Incorrect tax return

Inform Jakki of the following:

There may be interest and penalties if there is outstanding tax to pay on the income.

It is an offence not to tell HMRC about this information.

She should tell HMRC as soon as possible and pay any outstanding liabilities.

If she does not want to tell HMRC then her actions could be seen as money laundering.

We would have to cease acting for her.

Task 9

(a)

Asset	Chargeable	Exempt
Horse		✓ (wasting asset)
Field in which horse is kept	✓	
Antique horse brass costing £500, worth £1,700		✓ (exempt chattel -cost and proceeds < £6,000)

(b) The chargeable gain on sale is:

£	45,000

	£
Proceeds of sale	125,000
Less cost	(65,000)
enhancement expenditure	(15,000)
Chargeable gain	45,000

Redecoration is a revenue expense, not capital, and therefore not allowable.

(c) The allowable loss on sale is:

£	2,300

	£
Deemed disposal proceeds	6,000
Less disposal costs £(2,700 × 100/90) × 10%	(300)
Net proceeds	5,700
Less cost	(8,000)
Allowable loss	(2,300)

Task 10

Gain

	£
Proceeds of sale	8,000
Less cost	(1,250)
Chargeable gain	6,750

Share pool

	No of shares	Cost £
August 2009 Acquisition	2,000	5,000
September 2012 Bonus 1 for 1	2,000	0
	4,000	5,000
June 2016 Disposal (1,000/4,000 × £5,000)	(1,000)	(1,250)
c/f	3,000	3,750

Task 11

(a) The CGT payable for 2016/17 is:

£	689

	£
Gains	15,100
Less annual exempt amount	(11,100)
Taxable gains	4,000
CGT	
£1,110 (W) × 10%	111
£2,890 × 20%	578
CGT	689

(W) Unused basic rate band is £32,000 + £500 (£400 × 100/80) – £31,390 = £1,110

(b)

	✓
True	
False	✓

Provided the house has been occupied by the owner as his only or main residence at some time during the period of ownership, the last 18 months of ownership are exempt whether or not the owner lives in the house during that period.

Task 12

(a)

	✓
£28,250	
£31,250	
£29,750	✓
£23,800	

Workings:

	£
Gift	190,000
Less AE × 2 (16/17 + 15/16 b/f)	(6,000)
	184,000
Less nil rate band available (£325,000 – 260,000)	(65,000)
	119,000
IHT @ 20/80	£29,750

(b)

	✓
£123,000	
£27,000	
£66,000	✓
£18,000	

Workings:

	£
Before the gift: 100% shareholding 1,000 × £150	150,000
After the gift: 70% shareholding 700 × £120	(84,000)
Transfer of value	66,000

(c)

£	24,000

	£
House (net of mortgage) £(200,000 – 60,000)	140,000
Investments and cash	350,000
	490,000
Less funeral expenses	(5,000)
	485,000
Less exempt gift to spouse	(100,000)
Chargeable death estate	385,000
Less available nil rate band (no lifetime transfers)	(325,000)
	60,000
IHT @ 40%	24,000

Task 13

	£
Property	970,000
Building society deposits	387,000
Individual Savings Accounts	39,000
NS&I certificates	17,000
Proceeds of life policy	225,000
Gross estate	1,638,000
Less funeral expenses	(12,800)
loan	(1,200)
Net estate	1,624,000

	£
Inheritance tax	
£325,000 @ 0%	0
£1,299,000 @ 40%	519,600
Inheritance tax liability	519,600

Tax reference material FA 2016

Interpretation and abbreviations

Context

Tax advisers operate in a complex business and financial environment. The increasing public focus on the role of taxation in wider society means a greater interest in the actions of tax advisers and their clients.

This guidance, written by the professional bodies for their members working in tax, sets out the hallmarks of a good tax adviser, and in particular the fundamental principles of behaviour that members are expected to follow.

Interpretation

1.1 In this guidance:

- 'Client' includes, where the context requires, 'former client'.
- 'Member' (and 'members') includes 'firm' or 'practice' and the staff thereof.
- For simplicity, 'she' and 'her' are used throughout but should be taken to include 'he' and 'his'.
- Words in the singular include the plural and words in the plural include the singular.

Abbreviations

1.2 The following abbreviations have been used:

CCAB	Consultative Committee of Accountancy Bodies
DOTAS	Disclosure of Tax Avoidance Schemes
GAAP	Generally Accepted Accounting Principles
GAAR	General Anti-Abuse Rule in Finance Act 2013
HMRC	Her Majesty's Revenue & Customs
MLRO	Money Laundering Reporting Officer
NCA	National Crime Agency (previously the Serious Organised Crime Agency, SOCA)
POTAS	Promoters of Tax Avoidance Schemes
SRN	Scheme Reference Number

Fundamental principles

Overview of the fundamental principles

2.1 Ethical behaviour in the tax profession is critical. The work carried out by a member needs to be trusted by society at large as well as by clients and other stakeholders. What a member does reflects not just on themselves but on the profession as a whole.

2.2 A member must comply with the following fundamental principles:

Integrity

To be straightforward and honest in all professional and business relationships.

Objectivity

To not allow bias, conflict of interest or undue influence of others to override professional or business judgements.

Professional competence and due care

To maintain professional knowledge and skill at the level required to ensure that a client or employer receives competent professional service based on current developments in practice, legislation and techniques and acts diligently and in accordance with applicable technical and professional standards.

Confidentiality

To respect the confidentiality of information acquired as a result of professional and business relationships and, therefore, not disclose any such information to third parties without proper and specific authority, unless there is a legal or professional right or duty to disclose, nor use the information for the personal advantage of the member or third parties.

Professional behaviour

To comply with relevant laws and regulations and avoid any action that discredits the profession.

Each of these fundamental principles is discussed in more detail in the context of taxation services.

Tax return

Definition of tax return (return)

3.1 For the purposes of this chapter, the term 'return' includes any document or online submission of data that is prepared on behalf of the client for the purposes of disclosing to any taxing authority details that are to be used in the calculation of tax due by a client or a refund of tax due to the client or for other official purposes and, for example, includes:

- Self-assessment returns for income or corporation tax;
- VAT and Customs returns;
- PAYE returns;
- Inheritance tax returns;
- Returns or claims in respect of any other tax or duties where paid to the UK Government or any authority, such as a devolved government.

3.2 A letter giving details in respect of a return or as an amendment to a return including, for example, any voluntary disclosure on an error should be dealt with as if it was a return.

Taxpayer's responsibility

3.3 The taxpayer has primary responsibility to submit correct and complete returns to the best of her knowledge and belief. The return may include reasonable estimates where necessary. It follows that the final decision as to whether to disclose any issue is that of the client.

Member's responsibility

3.4 A member who prepares a return on behalf of a client is responsible to the client for the accuracy of the return based on the information provided.

3.5 In dealing with HMRC in relation to a client's tax affairs a member must bear in mind her duty of confidentiality to the client and that she is acting as the agent of her client. She has a duty to act in the best interests of her client.

3.6 A member must act in good faith in dealings with HMRC in accordance with the fundamental principle of integrity. In particular the member must take reasonable care and exercise appropriate professional scepticism when making statements or asserting facts on behalf of a client. Where acting as a tax agent, a member is not required to audit the figures in the books and records provided or verify information provided by a client or by a third party. A member should take care not to be associated with the presentation of facts she knows or believes to be incorrect or misleading nor to assert tax positions in a tax return which she considers have no sustainable basis.

3.7 When a member is communicating with HMRC, she should consider whether she needs to make it clear to what extent she is relying on information which has been supplied by the client or a third party.

Materiality

3.8 Whether an amount is to be regarded as material depends upon the facts and circumstances of each case.

3.9 The profits of a trade, profession, vocation or properly business must be computed in accordance with GAAP subject to any adjustment required or authorised by law in computing profits for those purposes. This permits a trade, profession, vocation or property business to disregard non-material adjustments in computing its accounting profits. However, it should be noted that for certain small businesses an election may be made to use the cash basis instead.

3.10 The application of GAAP, and therefore materiality, does not extend beyond the accounting profits. Thus the accounting concept of materiality cannot be applied when completing tax returns (direct and indirect), for example when:

- Computing adjustments required to accounting figures so as to arrive at taxable profits;
- Allocating income, expenses and outgoings across the relevant boxes on a self-assessment tax return;
- Collating the aggregate figures from all shareholdings and bank accounts for disclosure on tax returns.

Disclosure

3.11 If a client is unwilling to include in a tax return the minimum information required by law, the member should follow the guidance in Chapter 5 Irregularities. 3.12–3.18 give guidance on some of the more common areas of uncertainty over disclosure.

3.12 In general, it is likely to be in a client's own interests to ensure that factors relevant to her tax liability are adequately disclosed to HMRC because:

- Her relationship with HMRC is more likely to be on a satisfactory footing if she can demonstrate good faith in her dealings with them; and
- She will reduce the risk of a discovery or further assessment and may reduce exposure to interest and penalties.

3.13 It may be advisable to consider fuller disclosure than is strictly necessary. The factors involved in making this decision include:

- The terms of the applicable law;
- The view taken by the member;
- The extent of any doubt that exists;
- The manner in which disclosure is to be made; and
- The size and gravity of the item in question.

3.14 When advocating fuller disclosure than is strictly necessary a member should ensure that her client is adequately aware of the issues involved and their potential implications. Fuller disclosure should not be made unless the client consents to the level of disclosure.

3.15 Cases will arise where there is doubt as to the correct treatment of an item of income or expenditure, or the computation of a gain or allowance. In such cases a member ought to consider carefully what disclosure, if any, might be necessary. For example, additional disclosure should be considered where:

- A return relies on a valuation;
- There is inherent doubt as to the correct treatment of an item, for example, expenditure on repairs which might be regarded as capital in whole or part, or the VAT liability of a particular transaction; or
- HMRC has published its interpretation or has indicated its practice on a point, but the client proposes to adopt a different view, whether or not supported by Counsel's opinion. The member should refer to the guidance on the Veltema case and 3.19.

3.16 A member who is uncertain whether her client should disclose a particular item or of its treatment should consider taking further advice before reaching a decision. She should use her best endeavours to ensure that the client understands the issues, implications and the proposed course of action. Such a decision may have to be justified at a later date, so the members files should contain sufficient evidence to support the position taken, including contemporaneous notes of discussions with the client and/or with other advisers, copies of any second opinion obtained and the clients final decision. A failure to take reasonable care may result in HMRC imposing a penalty if an error is identified after an enquiry.

3.17 The 2012 case of *Charlton* clarified the law on discovery in relation to tax schemes disclosed to HMRC under DOTAS. The Upper Tribunal made dear that where the taxpayer has:

(i) Disclosed details of a significant allowable loss claim;

(ii) Declared relatively modest income/gains; and/or

(iii) Included the SRN issued by HMRC on the appropriate self-assessment tax return,an HMRC officer of reasonable knowledge and skill would be expected to infer that the taxpayer had entered into a tax avoidance scheme (and that fuller details of sat scheme would be contained in the relevant AAG1 Form). As a result HMRC would be precluded, in most cases, from raising a discovery assessment in a situation where the client implemented the disclosed scheme and HMRC failed to open an enquiry within the required time.

3.18 It is essential where a member is involved in the preparation of a self-assessment tax return which includes a scheme disclosed under DOTAS that the member takes care to ensure:

- That the tax return provides sufficient details of any transactions entered into (in case the AAG1 Form is incomplete);
- That the SRN is recorded properly in the appropriate box included for the purpose on a self-assessment tax return; and
- The SRN is shown for the self-assessment return for each year in which the scheme is expected to give the client a tax advantage.

Supporting documents

3.19 For the most part, HMRC does not consider that it is necessary for a taxpayer to provide supporting documentation in order to satisfy the taxpayer's overriding need to make a correct return. HMRC's view is that where it is necessary for that purpose, explanatory information should be entered in the 'white space' provided on the return. However, HMRC does recognise that the taxpayer may wish to supply further details of a particular computation or transaction in order to minimise the risk of a discovery assessment being raised at a later time.

3.20 Further HMRC guidance says that sending attachments with a tax return is intended for those cases where the taxpayer 'feels it is crucial to provide additional information to support the return but for some reason cannot utilise the white space'.

Approval of tax returns

3.21 It is essential that the member advises the client to review her tax return before it is submitted.

3.22 The member should draw the client's attention to the responsibility which the client is taking in approving the return as correct and complete. Attention should be drawn to any judgemental areas of positions reflected in the return to ensure that the client is aware of these and their implications before she approves the return.

3.23 A member should obtain evidence of the clients approval of the return in electronic or non-electronic form.

Tax advice

Introduction

4.1 Giving tax advice covers a variety of activities. It can involve advising a client on a choice afforded to her by legislation, for example, whether to establish a business as a sole trader, partnership or company. It could be advising on the tax implications of buying or selling an asset or business, or advising on succession planning.

4.2 For the most part clients are seeking advice on how to structure their affairs, either personal or commercial, in a way that is tax efficient and ensures that they comply with their legal and regulatory requirements. Transactions based on advice which are centred around non-tax objectives are less likely to attract scrutiny or criticism from stakeholders and are much mare likely to withstand challenge by HMRC.

4.3 Some tax strategies have been the subject of heated public debate, raising ethical challenges. Involvement in certain arrangements could subject the client and the member to significantly greater compliance requirements, scrutiny or investigation as well as criticism from the media, government and other stakeholders and difficulties in obtaining professional indemnity insurance cover.

4.4 The definition of 'avoidance' is an evolving area that can depend on the tax legislation, the intention of Parliament, interpretations in case law and the varying perceptions of different stakeholders and is discussed further below.

4.5 A member should consider the contents of this chapter carefully when giving tax advice and the potential negative impact other actions on the public perception of the integrity cite tax profession more generally.

4.6 Clearly a member must never be knowingly involved in tax evasion, although, of course, it is appropriate to act for a client who is rectifying their affairs.

Tax planning versus tax avoidance?

4.7 Despite attempts by courts over the years to elucidate tax 'avoidance' and to distinguish this from acceptable tax planning or mitigation, there is no widely accepted definition.

4.8 Publicly, the term 'avoidance' is used in the context of a wide range of activities, be it multinational structuring or entering contrived tax-motivated schemes. The application of one word to a range of activities and behaviours oversimplifies the concept and has led to confusion.

4.9 In a 2012 paper on tax avoidance, the Oxford University Centre for Business Taxation states that transactions generally do not fall into dear categories of tax avoidance, mitigation or planning. Similarly, it is often not clear whether something is acceptable or unacceptable. Instead the paper concludes that there is:

'a continuum from transactions that would not be effective to save tax under the law as it stands at present to tax planning that would be accepted by revenue authorities and courts without question.'

Member's responsibility in giving tax planning advice

4.10 A member is required to act with professional competence and due care within the scope of her engagement letter.

4.11 A member should understand her client's expectations around tax advice or tax planning, and ensure that engagement letters reflect the member's role and responsibilities, including limitations in or amendments to that role. The importance of this has been highlighted by the Mehjoo case.

4.12 A member does not have to advise on or recommend tax planning which she does not consider to be appropriate or otherwise does not align with her own business principles and ethics. However, in this situation the member may need to ensure that the advice she does not wish to give is outside the scope of her engagement. If the member may owe a legal duty of care to the client to advise in this area, the member should ensure that she complies with this by, for example, advising the client that there are opportunities that the client could undertake, even though the member is unwilling to assist, and recommending that the client seeks alternative advice. Any such discussions should be well documented by the member.

4.13 Ultimately it is the client's decision as to what planning is appropriate having received advice and taking into account their own broader commercial objectives and ethical stance. However, the member should ensure that the client is made aware of the risks and rewards of any planning, including that there may be adverse reputational consequences. It is advisable to ensure that the basis for recommended tax planning is clearly identified in documentation.

4.14 Occasionally a client may advise a member that she intends to proceed with a tax planning arrangement without taking full advice from her on the relevant issues or despite the advice the member has given. In such cases the member should warn the client of the potential risks of proceeding without full advice and ensure that the restriction in the scope of the member's advice is recorded in writing.

4.15 Where a client wishes to pursue a claim for a tax advantage which the member feels has no sustainable basis the member should refer to Chapter 5 Irregularities for further guidance.

4.16 If Counsel's opinion is sought on the planning the member should consider including the question as to whether, in Counsel's view, the GAAR could apply to the transaction.

4.17 It should be noted that any legal opinion provided, for example by Counsel, will be based on the assumptions stated in the instructions for the opinion and on execution of the arrangement exactly as stated. HMRC and the courts will not be constrained by these assumptions.

The different roles of a Tax Adviser

4.18 A member may be involved in tax planning arrangements in the following ways:

- Advising on a planning arrangement
- Introducing another advisers planning arrangement
- Providing a second opinion on a third party's planning arrangement
- Compliance services in relation to return which includes a planning arrangement

A member should always make a record of any advice given.

Irregularities

Introduction

5.1 For the purposes of this chapter, the term 'irregularity' is intended to include all errors whether the error is made by the client, the member, HMRC or any other party involved in a clients tax affairs.

5.2 In the course of a member's relationship with the client, the member may become aware of possible irregularities in the clients tax affairs. Unless already aware of the possible irregularities in question, the client should be informed as soon as the member has knowledge of them.

5.3 Where the irregularity has resulted in the client paying too much tax the member should advise the client about making a repayment claim and have regard to any relevant time limits. With the exception of this paragraph, the rest of this chapter deals solely with situations where sums may be due to HMRC.

5.4 On occasion, it may be apparent that an error made by HMRC has meant that the client has not paid tax actually due or she has been incorrectly repaid tax. Correcting such mistakes may cause expense to a member and thereby to her clients. A member should bear in mind that, in some circumstances, clients or agents may be able to claim for additional professional costs incurred and compensation from HMRC.

5.5 A member must act correctly from the outset. A member should keep sufficient appropriate records of discussions and advice and when dealing with irregularities the member should:

- Give the client appropriate advice;
- If necessary, so long as she continues to act for the client, seek to persuade the client to behave correctly;
- Take care not to appear to be assisting a client to plan or commit any criminal offence or to conceal any offence which has been committed; and
- In appropriate situations, or where in doubt, discuss the client's situation with a colleague or an independent third party.

5.6 Once aware of a possible irregularity, a member must bear in mind the legislation on money laundering and the obligations and duties which this places upon her.

5.7 A member should also consider whether the irregularity could give rise to a circumstance requiring notification to her professional indemnity insurers.

5.8 In any situation where a member has concerns about her own position, she should take specialist legal advice. This might arise, for example, where a client appears to have used the member to assist in the commission of a criminal offence in such a way that doubt could arise as to whether the member had acted honestly and in good faith.

5.9 The irregularity steps flowchart (5.10) summarises the recommended steps a member should take where a possible irregularity arises.

5.10 **Steps to take of there is a possible irregularity**

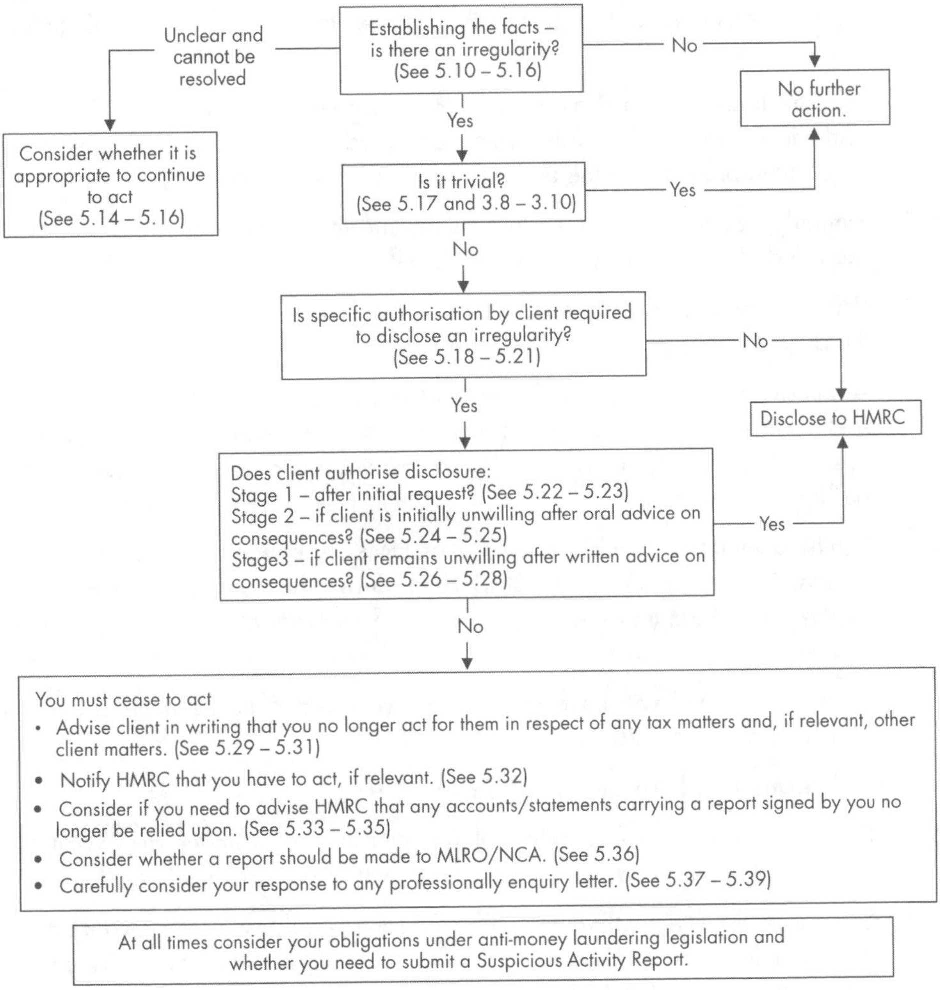

Access to data by HMRC

Introduction

6.1 For the purposes of this Chapter, the term 'data' includes documents in whatever form (including electronic) and other information. While this guidance relates to HMRC requests, other government bodies or organisations may also approach the member for data. The same principles apply.

6.2 A distinction must be drawn between a request for data made informally and those requests for data which are made in exercise of a power to require the provision of the data requested ('statutory requests').

6.3 Similarly, requests addressed to a client and those addressed to a member require different handling.

6.4 Where a member no longer acts for a client the member remains subject to the duty of confidentiality.

6.5 A member should comply with reasonable statutory requests and should not seek to frustrate legitimate requests for information. Adopting a constructive approach may help to resolve issues promptly and minimise costs to all parties.

6.6 Whilst a member should be aware of HMRC's powers in relation to the access, inspection and removal of data, given the complexity of the law relating to information powers, it may be appropriate to take specialist advice.

6.7 Revenue Scotland will have separate powers under the Revenue Scotland and Tax Powers Act 2014.

Informal request addressed to the member

6.8 Disclosure in response to informal request not made under any statutory power to demand data can only be made with client's permission.

6.9 Sometimes the client will have authorised routine disclosure of relevant data, for example, through the engagement latter. However, if there is any doubt about whether the client has authorised disclosure or about the accuracy of details, the members should ask the client to approve what is to be disclosed.

6.10 Where an oral enquiry is made by HMRC, a member should consider asking for it to be put in writing so that a response may be agreed with the client.

6.11 Although there is no obligation to comply with an informal request in whole or in part, a member should advise the client whether it is in the client's best interests to disclose such data.

6.12 Informal requests may be forerunners to statutory requests compelling the disclosure of data. Consequently, it may be sensible to comply with such requests or to seek to persuade HMRC that a more limited request is appropriate. The member should advise the client as to reasonableness of the informal request and likely consequences of not providing the data, so that the client can decide on her preferred course of action.

Informal requests addressed to the client

6.13 From time to time HMRC chooses to communicate directly with clients rather than with the appointed agent.

6.14 HMRC recognises the significant value which tax agents bring to both their clients and to the operation of the tax system. However, HMRC has also made it clear that on occasions it may deal with the taxpayers as well as, or instead of, the agent.

6.15 Examples of where HMRC may contact a member's client directly include:

- Where HMRC is using 'nudge' techniques to encourage taxpayers or claimants to re-check their financial records or to change behaviour.
- Where HMRC has become aware of particular assets, such as offshore investments, and the tax payer is encouraged to consider whether a further tax disclosure is required.
- Where the taxpayers has engaged in what HMRC considers to be a tax avoidance scheme, as HMRC considers that this will better ensure that the client fully understands HMRC's view.

6.16 HMRC has given reassurances that it is working to ensure that initial contact on compliance checks will normally be via the agent and only of the agent does not reply within an appropriate timescale will the contact be direct to the client.

6.17 When the member assists a client in dealing with such requests from HMRC, the member should apply the principles in 6.8–6.12.

Statutory requests addressed to the client

6.18 In advising the client a member should consider whether the notice is valid, how to comply the request and the consequences of non-compliance. Specialist advice may be needed, for example on such issues as whether the notice has been issued in accordance with the relevant tax legislation, whether the data requested is validly included in the notice, legal professional privilege and human rights.

6.19 Even if the notice is not valid, in may cases the client may conclude that the practical answer is to comply. If the notice is legally effective the client is legally obliged to comply with the request.

6.20 The member should also advise the client about any relevant right of appeal against the statutory request if appropriate and of the consequences of a failure to comply.

Statutory requests addressed to the member

6.21 The same principles apply to statutory request to the member as statutory requests to clients.

6.22 If a statutory request is valid it override the member's duty of confidentiality to her client.

6.23 In cases where the member is not legally precluded by the terms of the notice from communicating with the client, the members should advise the client of the notice and keep the client informed of progress and developments.

6.24 The member remains under a duty to preserve the confidentiality of her client so care must be taken to ensure that in complying with any notice the member does not provide or data outside the scope of the notice.

6.25 If a member is faced with a situation is which HMRC is seeking to enforce disclosure by the removal of data, the member should consider seeking immediate advice from a specialist adviser or other practitioner with relevant specialist knowledge, before permitting such removal, to ensure that this is the legally correct course of action.

6.26 Where a Schedule 36 notice is in point a member should note that it does not allow HMRC to inspect business premises occupied by a member in her capacity as an adviser. Specialist advice should be sought in any situation where HMRC asserts otherwise.

Privileged data

6.27 Legal privilege arises under common law and may only be overridden if this is expressly or necessarily implicitly set out in legislation. It protects a pates right to communicate in confidence with a legal adviser. The privilege belongs to the client and not to the member. If a document is privileged:

- The client cannot be required to make disclosure of that document to HMRC and a member should be careful to ensure that her reasons for advising a client nevertheless to make such a disclosure are recorded in writing
- It must not be disclosed by any other party, including the member, without the clients express permission

6.28 There are two types of legal privilege under common law, legal advice privilege covering documents passing between a client and her legal adviser prepared for the purposes of obtaining or giving legal advice and litigation privilege for data created for the dominant purpose of litigation. Litigation privilege may arise where litigation has not begun, but is merely contemplated and may apply to data prepared by non-lawyer advisers (including tax advisers) if brought into existence for the purposes of the litigation.

6.29 Communications from a tax adviser who is not a practising lawyer will not attract legal advice privilege but other similar protections exist under statute law, including:

- A privilege reporting exemption that applies to the reporting of money laundering in certain circumstances.
- A privilege under Schedule 36 whereby a tax adviser does not have to provide data that is her property and which constitute communications between the adviser and either her client or another tax adviser of the client. Information about such communications is similarly privileged. However, care should be taken as not all data may be privileged.

6.30 Whether data is or is not privileged and protected from the need to disclose is a complex issue, which will turn on the facts of the particular situation.

6.31 A member who receives a request for data, some of which she believes may be subject to privilege, should take independent legal advice on the position, unless expert in this area.

Tax tables 2016/2017

Tax rates and bands

Rates	Bands	Normal rates %	Dividend rates %
Basic rate	£1 – £32,000	20	7.5
Higher rate	£32,001 – £150,000	40	32.5
Additional rate	£150,001 and over	45	38.1

Personal allowances

		£
Personal allowance		11,000
Savings allowances:	Basic rate tax payer	1,000
	Higher rate tax payer	500
Dividend allowance		5,000
Income limit for personal allowances		100,000

Individual savings accounts

	£
Annual limit	15,240

Car benefit percentage

		%
Emissions for petrol engines:	0g/kilometre to 50g/km	7
	51g/km to 75g/km	11
	76g/km to 94g/km	15
	95g/km or more	16 + 1 for every extra 5g/km above 96g/km
Diesel engines		Additional 3%
Electric vehicles		7

Car fuel benefit

Car fuel benefit	£
Base figure	22,200

Approved mileage allowance payments

Mileage	Payment
First 10,000 miles	45p per mile
Over 10,000 miles	25p per mile
Additional passengers (per passenger)	5p per mile
Motorcycles	24p per mile
Bicycles	20p per mile

Van scale charge

	£
Basic charge	3,170
Private fuel charge	598
	%
Benefit charge for zero emissions vans	20

Non-taxable benefits

Staff party or event		£150 per head
Incidental overnight expenses:	Within the UK	£5 per night
	Overseas	£10 per night
Removal or relocation expenses		£8,000
Non-cash gifts from someone other than the employer		£250 per tax year
Staff suggestion scheme		Up to £5,000
Non-cash long service award		£50 per year of service

Work-related training courses		£15,480 per academic year
Health screening		1 per year
Mobile telephones		1 per employee
Childcare provision:	Basic rate taxpayer	£55 per week
	Higher rate taxpayer	£28 per week
	Additional rate taxpayer	£25 per week
Low-rate or interest free loans		Up to £10,000
Subsidised meal		£Nil
Provision of parking spaces		£Nil
Provision of workplace childcare		£Nil
Provision of workplace sports facilities		£Nil
Provision of eye tests and spectacles for VDU use		£Nil
Job-related accommodation		£Nil
Expensive accommodation limit		£75,000
Loan of assets annual charge		20%

HMRC official rate

HMRC official rate	3%

National insurance contributions

		%
Class 1 Employee:	£1 to £8,060	0
	£8,061 to £43,000	12
	£43,001 and above	2
Class 1 Employer:	£1 to 8,112	0
	£8,113 and above	13.8
Class 1A		13.8
		£
Employment allowance		3,000

Capital gains tax and tax rates

Capital gains tax	**£**
Annul exempt amount	11,100
Tax rates	**%**
Basic rate	10
High rate	20

Inheritance tax – tax rates

		%
£1 to £325,000		0
Excess:	Death rate	40
	Lifetime rate	20

Inheritance tax – taper relief

	% reduction
3 years or less	0
Over 3 years but less than 4 years	20
Over 4 years but less than 5 years	40
Over 5 years but less than 6 years	60
Over 6 years but less than 7 years	80

Inheritance tax – exemptions

		£
Small gifts		250 per transferee per tax year
Marriage or civil partnership:	From parent	5,000
	Grand parent	2,500
	One party to the other	2,500
	Others	1,000
Annual exemption		3,000

Notes

BPP
LEARNING MEDIA